# FOOD

## &

# FREEDOM

# FOOD

# & FREEDOM

## HOW THE SLOW FOOD MOVEMENT IS CHANGING THE WORLD THROUGH GASTRONOMY

# CARLO PETRINI

### Translated by JOHN IRVING

Rizzoli
*ex libris*

First published in the United States of America in 2015
by Rizzoli Ex Libris, an imprint of
Rizzoli International Publications, Inc.
300 Park Avenue South
New York, NY 10010
www.rizzoliusa.com

Originally published in Italy as Cibo e Libertà
Copyright © 2013 Giunti Editore S.p.A. Firenze - Milano
www.guinti.it
Copyright © 2013 Slow Food® Editore Srl
Via della Mendicità Istruita, 45 12042 Bra (Cn)
www.slowfood.it
Translation Copyright © 2015 John Irving

2015 2016 2017 2018 / 10 9 8 7 6 5 4 3 2 1

Distributed in the U.S. trade by Random House, New York

Printed in the U.S.A.

ISBN-13: 978-0-8478-4685-6

Library of Congress Catalog Control Number: 2015941947

RECYCLED
Paper made from
recycled material
FSC  FSC® C101537

# CONTENTS

## IV: The Gastronomy of Liberation

# PROLOGUE

**F**ood and Freedom—it's a challenging title! How often the word "freedom" has been misused down the centuries and is still misused today, usually irrelevantly, often contradictorily. I am not afraid of using it alongside the word "food," nor do I have any qualms about playing with it, as I do in the pages that follow. As the grandfather of the late Italian poet and screenwriter Tonino Guerra used to say, "I look backward to go forward." If I apply the same principle to the world of gastronomy, I see continuous liberations: liberations that have already happened and liberations—worthwhile, incredible, indispensable—that may happen in the future.

"Food" and "freedom," two words that have never been paired with as much pride as they are today. The centuries-old question of peasants, of the dignity of their labor and their struggles for the land comes to mind. In the early twentieth century, the Mexican Revolution was carried forward to the cry of "*¡Tierra y libertad!*" Today many processes of peacebuilding—the one underway in Colombia, for example—and of deep-reaching change are still going ahead in the name of the land. Yet something in the globalized panorama has altered profoundly: we are now living in a schizophrenic dimension in which the rural world and the use of land, the two fundamental elements for feeding people, are at the mercy of a system in which food has lost all its complex values and become a commodity that makes sense only as a function of its price. Food is now a product subject to all sorts of speculation. Instead of reducing the problems of the majority of the world population, increased food production has aggravated them and even generated new ones. The most glaring proof of this is the fact that hunger and nutrition have not gone away, while pollution and depletion of resources are multiplying and, save for a few exceptions, farmers continue to be the "fifth wheel on the wagon," even if they do own the land they cultivate. The battle for freedom is no longer being fought over the land alone. For the new era and for the new battles ahead, the Mexican Revolution cry of "*¡Tierra y libertad!*" might justifiably be changed into "*¡Cibo y libertad!*"—food and freedom.

Food is thus becoming an instrument of liberation. I say this in light of the many stories that touch me personally insofar as they relate the adventure of Slow Food and Terra Madre, and as such are by no means a small part of my own life. In this book I have tried to reconstruct a journey based on my own experience and on the encounters and meetings I have had along the way. The leading players are thus other people: people involved in Slow Food and Terra Madre and people who, in one way or another, have tuned into them from the outside. It is a journey that set out from my home turf—Bra, a small town in the northwestern Italian region of Piedmont—in the 1980s. After ranging far and wide, it has led me to a vision of future prospects so broad that they embrace the whole world.

I begin by speaking about the liberations that have already been achieved, from the one I define as *gastronomia liberata*,[1] liberated gastronomy, partly to endow it with scientific dignity, partly to convey its importance as a holistic, complex set of ideas and sensibilities, of relations and connections, as a new intellectual perspective for material culture, built up through many minor liberations and capable today of releasing—indeed, of liberating!—extraordinary energy. Even the tools it uses have

---

[1] For the Italian ear, the locution playfully evokes *Gerusalemme liberata*, an epic poem by Torquato Tasso (1544–1595), traditionally translated into English, however, as *Jerusalem Delivered* [*translator's note*].

to be freed. It is necessary to *liberate diversity* as an increasingly effective element of extraordinary creativity, ensuring that the new networks that are now making the world go around assume the characteristics of an unconditionable free network, like the one I have built with my traveling companions at Slow Food and Terra Madre.

All this can be harnessed to develop projects that are certainly ambitious—some might say too ambitious—but can no longer be delayed if we are to achieve what is ultimately the most important liberation of all.

I refer to gastronomy, which, having been liberated, is now becoming the gastronomy "of liberation." The process has taken place over four stages, which I enjoyed traveling through and which I relive again in this book. *The gastronomy of liberation*: it is a slogan that came to mind looking at Latin America and what is happening over there, which I find thrilling. In Latin America, in fact, I have at last seen the fruits of work whose roots were laid a long way back in time. Anyone unfamiliar with the history of the movement I represent and all the humanity who, for whatever reason, take part in it may find this hard to believe. Liberation, at last, from the most scandalous of yokes and cages: inequality, oppression, the damage it wreaks on the environment and people, the scandal of hunger and malnutrition.

I realize this affirmation may sound pretentious and gratuitously rhetorical, but I am convinced it is true, and I would like you, too, to follow the route that has led me to pronounce it in such a peremptory fashion. The subject in question is, of course, very complex, but the places and the people involved, their activities and their stories, which I recount here, make it clearer and help us understand its ins and outs. It will not be easy to achieve our goal, but in the story you are about to read, few things were easy at the time and no one was overly frightened. After all, we are not alone: all together, we can make it happen.

# I. LIBERATED GASTRONOMY

## CHAPTER I

# IN THE BEGINNING WAS WINE

**B**eppe Colla was the president of the Barolo Barbaresco Protection Consortium at the time. It was just after the famous "methanol scandal," in which fraudulent winemakers had boosted the alcohol content of their wine by blending it with toxic methanol.[2] I can still see Beppe's face as he wept on my television screen. Proud but forlorn, he simply could not hold back his tears. It was early April 1986, and at that moment in time it looked like "game over" for the entire Italian wine sector. What with customs clampdowns and a declining public image, the year eventually ended with a 37 percent fall in wine exports and the loss of a quarter of its total value for the whole wine sector. It was

---

[2] In 1986, wine adulterated with methanol produced at the Ciravegna cellar in Narzole, in the province of Cuneo, caused the death by intoxication of twenty-three people in the north of Italy and the blinding of others. In 1992, the Italian Supreme Court handed down definitive sentences against eleven defendants, four of whom were convicted of murder.

no joke living through it all, a stone's throw away from so many wine producer friends in Piedmont's Langa wine district. Beppe Colla's public tears were a sign not only of despair for the intolerable shame of the scandal—not to mention the likelihood of huge economic losses—but also of much more than that. Today, thirty years on, I can see it all more clearly.

The disaster, which caused twenty-three deaths and changed Italian wine forever, laid bare connections that had hitherto been invisible to most people. It affected the lives of thousands of good producers, people who had invested their entire existences in winemaking. Having mixed with them on a regular basis for years, and after developing a passion for wine tasting in the late 1970s, I was close to many. They were all very forthright people with all the qualities and defects you would associate with farmers. I often used to meet up with them, to go see them in their cellars and vineyards. Sipping and comparing the oldest vintages and tracing their evolution through time over a delicious homemade salami, say, or a steaming dish of *tajarin*, our local version of egg tagliatelle, kneaded and cut by the cook of the house the same morning, we would mull over the concept of terroirs and the future of our wine and food.

Meetings between wine producers and the early collaborators of Arcigola, the first "version" of Slow Food that officially came into being in the summer of 1986, were like the gatherings of an inner circle of dreamers. We had a whale of a time enjoying the gastronomic gems of our local area, and we also knew exactly what we were talking about. The scandal of methanol-tainted wine had forced Italy to face the fact that winemaking was not only part and parcel of an important economic sector with potential fallouts in others. It was also, more importantly, closely intertwined with the lives of people ruined by the speculation of a bunch of crooks who had been adulterating wine with methyl alcohol—from which, needless to say, the tax had just been lifted.

The lives of the people who grew grapes and made wine were also the lives of those local areas: their fertility, their social fabric, their culture, their ecosystems.

Seeing how they helped reawaken our senses, we had initially regarded our wine tastings as revolutionary. But in that particular historical context, they now seemed to be verging on the absurd. What was the point of splitting hairs over an aroma or a scent or a color in the glass, if in the meantime the bond between wine and the local area and the real lives of real people was being broken? If everything could be polluted, adulterated, violated?

As if that weren't enough, two other dramatic and revealing events brought us clattering down to earth from our flights of fancy and of taste in that spring of 1986. At the end of April, in fact, came the Chernobyl nuclear accident. Market traders and wholesalers still measure disastrous years against that summer's drop in sales. We had to stop eating salads and avoided fresh vegetables in general. The salubriousness of fish and meat was also called into question. In those days, ecology was still shrouded in an almost sectarian aura as the preserve of narrow "non-aligned" cliques, but it was also very much bound up with food. And as if to prove the point, one atrazine pollution emergency followed another in the Po Valley well into the autumn. The taps in many houses had to be turned off at the mains and the cause of contaminated aqueducts was soon identified: the indiscriminate use of pesticides in agriculture.

During that spring, new connections revealed themselves to us self-taught gastronomes, lovers of material culture, pioneers of the right to pleasure, who a few months later were to found Arcigola, and then, a few years later, Slow Food. New points of view were breaking free from the cages of thought that were subsequently to run off in the most disparate directions, just like the leading players of that period, who fell apart only to join together again with new ideas and the foundations for newer ideas still.

With hindsight, it is easier of course to connect events, but one cannot help noting how it was the climate and the events of those months that released the new energies that are still making the food revolution happen: a slow revolution, which, like every revolution in history, violent or otherwise, conveys a form of liberation.

In this case, it is gastronomy that has liberated itself from the restrictions imposed by people who judged by mere appearances—and there are still many of them around—people who simply confined themselves to judging the end results of processes as complex as the ones that turn nature into food: a wine, a product, a dish cooked by a chef. This restriction was born of the mechanistic separation of disciplines and fed by hedonism as an end to itself; it was a cage that held gastronomic science prisoner. In those days, no one ever talked about gastronomy as a science. The last to do so had been Jean-Anthelme Brillat-Savarin a century and a half earlier, in 1825, in his *Physiologie du goût*. Now, all these years later, it was urgent to reformulate the science to render it holistic, interdisciplinary, capable of embracing all the learning but also all the life concealed behind every item of food. It was more than a matter of taste for now, in the face of the drama of winemakers brought to their knees by the methanol scandal, it was inconceivable merely to taste wine. It was more than a matter of economics, too, since seeing gastronomy solely from the business point of view is a function of brainlessness, as is swooning over an aroma of woodland fruits or the bouquet of Sauvignon, which typically smacks of cat's piss. The more people lost their brains—and many still do—over the aesthetic aspects of food and wine, the more they received body blows (always dealt, incidentally, by others with money and their own interests at heart). Ultimately, methanol was being put into wine because wine had begun to cost less. Otherwise it would not have been economical to adulterate such a precious fruit—and also one of the symbols—of our local area.

That summer spent in wine cellars in 1986 was one of the mainsprings of our decision to say that enough was enough. We had reached the stage where we wanted to think about food in its entirety, taking into account everything about it, across the board, from the people to the places behind it, from its productive processes to its cultural implications. We wanted to improve quality, cultivating it with the wine producers for whom it was a banner and a lifestyle. We wanted to learn to recognize it and promote it, to find out more about it and calibrate it to a formula—"good, clean, and fair"—which at that time existed only *in nuce* and would only be formally defined and put down on paper a couple of decades later. It is a formula that has liberated gastronomy—hitherto relegated to gourmets whose sole concern was to decide what was good and what was not—more than just theoretically. But have we liberated it entirely? The answer is no, since there are still a great many people wandering around in gastronomic straitjackets—everyone's entitled to enjoy themselves as they see fit, after all. Some of them are enthralled by the collective folly that is the explosion of food in the media, especially in television programs that, at all hours of the day and on every channel, burst at the seams with the stuff in a form that I do not hesitate to define as pornographic. Pornography is sex without sentiment, right? It may of course be enjoyable, just like food eaten without awareness and, to put it bluntly, without a modicum of sentiment for all the humanity behind the processes and actions and thoughts that bring it to the table. Sentiment like the compassion I still feel today for Beppe Colla, the man who wept in front of the whole of Italy, the representative of a wine world that, fortunately, has grown up a lot since then, as has a large section of our country's farming and all of its gastronomy. Maybe we and everyone else who has embraced complexity have grown up a little, too.

# CHAPTER 2

# TOURING THE COUNTRY

Luigi Veronelli[3] used to like speaking and, above all, writing about "touring osterias," "touring wine cellars," "touring the countryside." He was one of the masters to whom my generation of gastronomes—hence, indirectly, the generations that have followed, too—owes the flowering of their passion, the urge to go out and explore, the credit for their discoveries. We immediately saw that beloved expression of his as a mission.

First, though, came education. We needed to understand, to train our senses to recognize the characteristics of each food and, as we soon realized, everything about it, behind it, and before it; namely local context, humanity, and future potential. I had attended the exacting tasting courses at the Ecole des Vins de Bourgogne in Beaune, in Burgundy, and in the first half of

---

[3] Luigi Veronelli (1926–2004) was an Italian enologist, cook, gastronome, writer, and journalist famous for his wine and restaurant guides.

the 1990s, I completed my training with the courses Massimo Martinelli used to run in the municipal wine cellar at La Morra, a village near my home. Well-trained senses waiting to be cultivated, ready to assimilate different flavors and different realities—this was the main baggage I began to carry with me, first in the Langa hills, then through the whole of Italy. Eager to explore landscapes, vineyards, wine cellars, winemakers, differences between terrains and the people who worked them, we would set off in cars that were to grow less and less beat-up and battered in the course of time. We would take the longest, most inconvenient, and, fortunately, slowest detours to sit at the tables we had read and heard about from masters and friends, to swap views with legendary restaurateurs, to discover new osterias that producers had told us about. Sometimes we would skip lunch or, at the most, wolf down a grilled sandwich, to be able to afford a better dinner. In our notebooks and tasting notes, the number of the cellars we had visited, the tables we had eaten at, and the people involved in gastronomy we had met was growing all the time. Our network of friends was expanding, as was the number of Arcigola's members. We always used to take a carbon-copy card book on our travels to enroll new members.

We were touring the Italian countryside and lapping up its material culture. Drinking and eating in the places where wine and food were produced with the people who had produced them was changing our perspective. Veronelli-style "touring" was proving to be a way of liberating gastronomy from the constraint of pleasure as an end to itself, as an elitist and, at best, snobbish self-compulsion with respect to the work of the people who created all that bounty, with respect to their care and attention for the places in which they grew and bred and processed it. Maybe we were still not entirely conscious of the fact at the time, but by meeting with farmers and restaurateurs and winegrowers in their own homes, we were revolutionizing gastronomy. Two centuries on from its birth in its modern form, it meant setting gastronomy free to embrace other fundamental elements of our existence, such as sociality and conviviality, the salubriousness of the air, water, and soil, memory and history, the survival and preservation of our local areas, such as beauty and good living in the fullest sense of the term, and learning no longer hamstrung by the fierce speculation that reigns in the official temples of knowledge.

On our travels, Gigi Piumatti (later to become editor of the *Italian Wines* guide published first by Arcigola, then from 1988 to 2009 by Slow Food Editore in conjunction with Gambero Rosso) and I used the *Catalogo Bolaffi dei vini d'Italia*, edited by who else but Veronelli, as our guide, and that is how we came to make the personal acquaintance of all the great Italian winemakers. Alternating interminable shifts at the wheel, we drove right to the bottom of the Italian boot, and as we went the trunk of the car gradually filled up with purchases and primary ingredients for the events and tastings we were organizing for Arcigola: from the *Comizi agrari* (agrarian councils) to the International Convention of Piedmontese Wine in 1990, two milestones that marked a break with the past. We met some of the grand old men of Italian wine, generally gruff types who would only open up when they had ascertained that our passion was genuine and that we actually did possess the rudiments of real knowledge. In Piedmont they encouraged us to collect interviews and draw up maps of the geographical boundaries between crus, sorì in local dialect, which proved useful a few years later when we published the first and only *Wine Atlas of the Langhe: The Great Barolo and Barbaresco Vineyards* (Arcigola Slow Food Editore, 1990). We also bumped into the grand young men, the new generation who, often at loggerheads with their fathers, were to be the leading players in the renaissance that followed the methanol scandal. The second half of the 1980s and the early 1990s were a wonderful period:

Barolo and Barbaresco from the Langa hills were beginning to compete with the world's great wines, especially French ones, while Tuscany was bursting with quality wine and legendary labels. Thanks to brilliant, enlightened producers, other regions were also setting out on a journey that, in many cases, was to take them into the international limelight. The pursuit of quality, at first sporadic, was allowing previously disregarded or unknown grape varieties to express their full potential, swaying palates at every latitude and lavishing opportunities and economic well-being on the very winemakers who had stared disaster in the face in 1986.

It is fundamental to remember Italian enology's very rapid rise from quasi-anonymity to success, as this, too, was a liberation. Indeed, it was arguably the very first, the one from which others sprang: liberation *from* poverty (in the Langa hills in particular, memories of the hardships suffered by their peasant fathers and mothers in wartime and after still lingered on in everyone) and poor, precarious living conditions, but also liberation *of* new energies. Repudiation of pleasure as an end in itself and acknowledgment of the success of the local area and its people as an integral part of a wine's value—why, we began to ask ourselves, shouldn't the same happen for a ham or a bread, for a native fruit or vegetable species, for a cheese? Which is why on our travels we would also end up meeting pork butchers, bakers, gardeners, dairymen, and shepherds. We organized comparative food tastings along the lines of wine tastings, we took these people to present their produce to gourmets and anyone else who might be interested, sometimes people who would sign up for events simply to enjoy a good feed, but eventually went home with new notions in their heads, ideas to pass on in their own local contexts, all the makings of a new passion, and, maybe, even a new way of thinking about food—and of eating it.

Touring the countryside no longer meant touring vineyards alone, it also meant touring the whole land. Gastronomy was being liberated and ideas that had lain dormant for more than a hundred years—ever since gastronomic science's debut with Brillat-Savarin—were now reappearing afresh. How reductive it was of us to limit ourselves, like well-mannered, sentient animals, to the act of tasting alone without combining it with complete, complex knowledge of local areas. Guzzling was no longer gratifying and the meaning of the term "bon vivant" was changing. It was no longer enough simply to "tour" restaurants as the majority of self-styled gastronomes used to do.

It was necessary to break the bars of the cage and explain to everyone—especially those who should have been addressing the matter as part of their institutional mission—about the treasure that was lying dormant a few kilometers from our homes, often inside our towns and villages. As for pleasure, there was nothing more pleasurable and liberating than this new, deeper form of conviviality, than watching a close-knit fabric of human relations grow in Italy and the world, than the sharing of ideas and projects. It was what we would one day come to call a "network."

# CHAPTER 3

# MILANO GOLOSA

**W**riting in *Corriere della sera* on November 23, 1994, Marisa Fumagalli described Milano Golosa (Greedy Milan), an event scheduled to be held a few days later, as follows:

Down with top models, up with bottles. For once parading on the catwalk we won't be seeing Claudia, Cindy and Naomi but Barolo, Malvasia and Pinot Noir . . . It'll be a Milan good enough to drink (and to eat),[4] the city that for four days will be hosting a veritable show of taste centered around hundreds of tastings of great wines, Italian and international, and gastronomic products from all over the world in a succession of "workshops" where it will be possible to sample the most fanciful food combina-

---

[4] "Milan good enough to drink." A rendering of *Milano da bere*, the slogan of a 1985 Amaro Ramazzotti TV commercial subsequently taken up by journalists and in popular culture to describe the city's prosperity and fashion world in the 1980s.

tions and the rarest wines. Don't be misled by the famous 1980s commercial, though. Remember it? The advertising slogan for a famous drink soon became the symbol of a certain lifestyle concerned most of all with appearance [ . . . ] in short, it's an invite to "food meditation." Which is at odds with speed, chasing time, the obsessive pace we've grown accustomed to [ . . . ] Milano Golosa is giving it a go [ . . . ] Here are a few of the most tempting Taste Workshops topics: "The Aristocratic Pleasure of Sachertorte" (four of Milan's most prestigious confectioners offer their take on the Viennese original); "Taste of Smoke . . . Taste of the Sea" (smoked salmon, sturgeon, swordfish, eel and trout matched with great wines); "Wines From Another World" (meetings, curiosities and surprises to discover the new production of Chile, Australia, New Zealand and South Africa).

I want to commit to memory that defining event, organized in Milan from December 1 to 4 at Industria e Superstudio—1,200 square meters of former industrial floor space in the city's Porta Genova neighborhood—in collaboration with the company then spearheaded by the famous "gastronaut" and journalist Davide Paolini: first, because it established the success of the Taste Workshops formula, Slow Food's original, codified way of speaking about gastronomy and popularizing new trends in the production world; second, because I remember an inaugural speech of mine based on an analogy precisely with the world of fashion.

I argued that the dark ages had come to an end for food and wine, in Italy a business sector as important as fashion, if not more. I said that the day food was spoken about in the same way as fashion would mark a notable step forward for the whole country. The remark caused some perplexity, with some people mistaking it for provocation by a pleasure-seeking glutton.

In actual fact, the situation was still grim; the methanol scandal had happened almost ten years before, but there was still a long way to go. Food on television was a subject of fleeting interest, well treated but confined to a niche, the Internet was in its early days, almost all true Italian gastronomes knew each other, and many, myself included, were not immune from naiveté (for example, we had no idea then that the consumption of wild salmon and swordfish was slowly leading to the extinction of these species). But in 1994, we were more convinced than we had ever been—we were not joking. The time had come to acknowledge that the food and wine sector was one of the pillars of our "Italianness," of our way of working and living—something important on which we could lay the bases for a better future. It was necessary to become aware of the sector's economic and cultural value, to stop regarding it as a piece of fun—as a hobby for hedonists and nothing more—with the almost onanistic ostentation that had long branded the public image of the gastronome (this is still an open problem and we are still the butt of similar prejudices today). Between the 1980s and 1990s, it was an image that sat well with the reigning yuppiedom, especially, needless to say, in Milan.

Yet, precisely in Milan, the Milano Golosa event was an act of liberation. We might define it today as our "Four Days of Milan."[5] Paying an admission fee of 40,000 lire entitled you to choose from the ninety workshops, tastings, and courses slated each day. Here was a new way of approaching tasting: the Taste Workshops, a formula first introduced earlier the same year as part of Slow Food's participation at the Vinitaly wine and spirits exhibition in Verona, were a very powerful tool for achieving the main aim of our "association"—namely taste education. The philosophy and method with which we still organize them at all our events—with

---

[5] A reference to the Five Days of Milan, an event that took place in 1848, when five days of rebellion against the Austrian rulers of the city triggered the First Italian War of Independence.

attractive titles, a fun style, and a dash of razzmatazz—testify to our desire to relate directly with producers and experts. The *Dizionario di Slow Food*, published by Slow Food Editore in 2002, describes "Taste Workshops" as "the desire to break free from the everyday chore/necessity of eating and drinking to charge the gesture of taking food to the mouth with different cultural and symbolic significances." The entry goes on as follows:

> A concrete and conscious experience: an opportunity to acquire knowledge of techniques and the cultural context in which a food product or a wine or a dish is born, a chance to learn (or elaborate) the language of tasting. Not just an act of hedonism or an academic practice, but a moment of material culture, a pleasurable meeting with food and wine of the highest quality. Not a technical tasting in which scores are assigned to establish scales of value or determine standards of quality, but, above all else, a pleasurable experience.

The presenters of these meetings, often assisted by food and wine producers and experts, describe food products from the commodity, productive, and sensory point of view, and from that of their place of origin. Here is a way of spreading knowledge with a new language, stimulating curiosity and communicating the need to defend biodiversity. The public at Milano Golosa experienced a new way of eating and drinking and talking about food. The evocative power, cultural significance, and economic importance of Italian food and drink were at last appearing on an important international stage (the products showcased were not only Italian), stimulating original new ideas and releasing energies. Milano Golosa's amazing success encouraged us to develop this event model, and two years later, we translated it into the Salone del Gusto in Turin. Above all, it marked the moment in time in which all the work we had done to dignify gastronomy—to extend its field of action and interest—began to become popular and attract enthusiastic support.

The "Four Days of Milan" pushed the process of liberation of gastronomy to a point of no return. Today food has become comparable to fashion in the way it is talked about in the media and everyday conversation. Though this may be gratifying for those of us who predicted it in 1994, by contrast all this attention fails to acknowledge our somewhat wider, indeed holistic, productive vision and our awareness of our limits.

# CHAPTER 4

# ECO-
# GASTRONOMY

On December 9, 2001, the *New York Times* published an article by Lawrence Osborne entitled "The Year in Ideas: A to Z." Under the letter "S," Osborne speaks about Slow Food. It was by no means the first time the authoritative American daily had mentioned us. In around 2000, in fact, it had come up with an interesting neologism to define us: a movement of "eco-gastronomes," it called us. A year later, Osborne was describing us as follows:

> The Slow Food movement, which is just now making inroads in America, is a gastronomic version of Greenpeace: a defiant determination to preserve unprocessed, time-intensive food from being wiped off the culinary map. And like anti-W.T.O. activism, the movement is a protest against globalism. But Slow Food activism doesn't take the form of street demonstrations. Instead, activists are encouraged to savor organic cabbages and dissect the joys of truffles in their kitchens. Protest was never this much fun.

These are words that still make me smile, because, though they capture interesting characteristics of Slow Food, they also induce somewhat naive errors of evaluation. I have now gotten used to the fact that when one decides to regard gastronomy as a science as complex as the world itself, it is highly likely that one's actions and thoughts will be wrongly interpreted or misunderstood. It is likelier still if, on account of their background and *forma mentis*, the person judging makes no attempt to conceive the great complexity of food. The *New York Times* article speaks at once of rebellion, protest, and fun, of taste and activism. This is in itself an interesting point and, to some extent, it hits the nail on the head. Yet the whole article is permeated by a vaguely supercilious tone, recounting the Slow Food movement almost as if it were a curiosity of globalism and postmodernism, a sort of object of mystery to be observed with affection. As if to say, "Let's see how far these crazy folks will go."

Osborne writes that Slow Food is against globalism, mistaking our interest in local areas and the promotion of the local economic scale for something incompatible with globalization. Wrong.

He speaks of dissecting the joys of truffles in the kitchen, mistaking the typical Taste Workshop approach for a playful twist on marginal questions of existence. Wrong again.

The reason he uses organic cabbages as an example is that in that period in the United States, a network of organics-conscious producers and consumers was coming to the fore. This was an experience that, albeit verging on the obsessive in some extreme cases, was nonetheless another important form of liberation. It has now reached previously unthinkable dimensions, so much so that it has profoundly changed the diet of millions of North Americans. This is a subject I shall come back to later.

Osborne talks of preferences for non-processed foods, which would seem to suggest an inclination toward the natural or at least conveys an aversion on our part toward all processed food. True only in part.

His reference, finally, to "time-intensive food" really is the fruit of a mechanistic, schematic *modus pensandi*, as if a food can be judged according to how long it takes to prepare, process, and consume. It is no coincidence that in the early days, when we used to travel abroad to promote Slow Food in non-English-speaking countries, one of the recurring questions was: "What do you do with Slow Food? Do you have to sit at the table for hours? Have you only to cook long, complicated recipes?" Literally translated, the name Slow Food—*alimentation lente, manger lentement, comida lenta, cibo lento*—may of course be misleading. I used to see this as a positive: at least we would not be pigeonholed only in contrast with fast food. We were rousing curiosity and there was scope for work on a different concept of food and a new gastronomic *science*.

Most interestingly, the *New York Times* article represents Slow Food as "a gastronomic version of Greenpeace." This may be a slight exaggeration, but it does capture an aptitude and a philosophy that we have developed over the years. Our defense of the right to pleasure against the standardization of taste through a new approach to tasting, our tours of the country, and the succession of food scandals and ecological disasters had ultimately convinced us that a gastronome who consumes the produce of the land cannot remain insensitive to environmental issues. In 2001 at the first Slow Food USA congress, held in a splendidly restored wooden hayloft in Bolinas, California, I began my speech with the words, "A gastronome who is not an environmentalist is surely stupid, but an environmentalist who is not a gastronome is merely sad!" Our American members couldn't stop laughing. For good measure I used the image of gastronomes emptying their glasses and filling their bellies with every goodie imaginable in the restaurant car of a train speeding toward an abyss with no one there to stop it. That train was this earth of ours, which has to be tended and saved, its food first and foremost. The time had come to break free from the "pen" in which people "dissected the joys of truffle," to jump out of the restaurant car.

We took to the term "eco-gastronomy" immediately. Maybe our environmentalist friends were less keen, most likely seeing it as a way of trespassing on their property or, even worse, of giving their mission an aura of playfulness and frivolity unbefitting serious militants. But being serious does not necessarily mean harming oneself and shunning pleasure. The neologism said something immediately perceivable about our gastronomic approach, sensitive to economic problems on a global scale, to the profound changes that the rural world was undergoing at every latitude, to the urgent need to safeguard biodiversity. But it took some time—and I have the impression it will take more still—to make people realize that pleasure is also tied to these closely interconnected questions. Yet, though these connections came to the fore in the mid-1980s, they are still invisible to many.

The annoyance of many environmentalists is indicative of how the process of liberation had already begun for gastronomy. They, the ecological caste, on the other hand, were digging in, often confining themselves to protest without appreciating the liberating value of the meeting between different disciplines and fields of knowledge. This was odd for people who saw the environment as a banner to fight for, since there is nothing more complex and interrelated than an ecosystem. I hope environmentalists will not be angry with me, as I actually feel great sympathy for them, but when a movement obstinately locks itself up in its own specifics, it is over before it has even begun. Italian voters perceived this clearly and, as a result, environmental issues virtually disappeared from the political debate and from institutional tables. In Italy, ecology is often just another "enclosure."

Let me add that I also noted a certain dismay among many early "slowfoodies" and fellow gastronomes who felt—though some were to change their minds years later—or still feel that gastronomy should not extend its field of action this far, that responsibility toward the environment and socioeconomic issues is antithetical to the pleasure of fine dining. Faced with the choice, they preferred to opt for the latter. As did many important cooks and chefs, convinced that their (unquestionable) mastery was capable of transforming any food product of any origin, whatever its heritage, into perfection.

I believe that they were wrong and that history is beginning to prove me right. In the late 1990s, the way to a holistic conception of food, hence, to use Brillat-Savarin's celebrated definition, "of all that relates to man as a feeding animal," was already laid. Even as the "liberated gastronomy" movement was propelling us into terrains that would have been unthinkable at the outset, we were refining our thinking still further.

# CHAPTER 5
# GCF

**B**uono, *pulito e giusto*, "Good, clean, and fair"—when my friend and collaborator Carlo Bogliotti and I came up with this title for the book we were working on in 2005, subsequently published at the end of the same year by the Turin publisher Einaudi (translated in English as *Slow Food Nation: Why Our Food Should be Good, Clean, and Fair*, Rizzoli Ex Libris, New York, 2007) we were standing in the courtyard of my house in Bra. We were using all the spare time we had to figure out how to finally make the Slow Food philosophy more organic. In the course of twenty years it had evolved so much—and grown more complicated. So even walking home from the office, we would continue to work, talking nonstop. When our meditations yielded the little slogan "Good, clean, and fair," we turned our noses up at it at first. It struck us as being banal.

"It'll never work," we said and we shelved it, though it did continue to linger in the background as a guiding thread for the structure of the book. But when publication time arrived, of all the titles possible we chose it, *Buono, pulito e giusto*, the one that had initially seemed so unsuitable. How wrong we were! It was eventually well received by the whole Slow Food movement and has become the slogan-cum-banner of our association. It has since come in handy for communication among ourselves and also proved useful for publicizing the events we organize, for further refining our philosophy and ordering our thoughts and actions. Above all, it has traveled around the world in different languages. "Good, clean, and fair" is catchy: you can hear it at U.S. farmers' markets; it stood out on a huge banner they unfurled to welcome me to an elementary school in Kenya; I have seen it in Japanese and Korean ideograms; "*Bueno, limpio y justo*" is the rallying cry of the *campesinos* of the Terra Madre food communities in South America. I was almost moved to tears when I saw it daubed in paint on huts in a village in the Mexican state of Chiapas, with a huge picture of a *caracol*, the Slow Food snail symbol, next to it. In France, "*Bon, propre et juste*" is arguably better known than the movement itself. The slogan has now transcended the Slow Food galaxy to become almost a figure of speech. I see it in the most unlikely places and contexts and I detect traces of it in certain food advertising campaigns, which, though they may not dare to cite it explicitly, undoubtedly hint at it. Sometimes it is also used disparagingly or derisorily in criticisms leveled at Slow Food or anyone else who has more than a mere narcissistic or aesthetic taste for food at heart: for example, the practitioners of organics, good practices, the fight against waste, and social justice in the agrifood sector. Thanks to the immediacy that we, in the courtyard of my house that day, had mistaken for banality, the title has evidently hit the mark.

The subtitle of the book, *Princîpi di una nuova gastronomia* (Principles of a new gastronomy), was meant to be anything but banal and raised the bar a little higher. It was born of a desire to put down in writing a redefinition of this field of knowledge as a fully fledged science—an inexact one maybe, but with little to envy other human sciences deemed academically "more noble." Has all this served to make gastronomy a liberated science? The GCF triptych has largely done the job, the "principles" arguably less so. I say this because I realize that, while the title of the book has caught on more than we would ever have imagined, much of the content has yet to be put fully into practice, the plan it proposed in particular. I occasionally go back to the book and I am always surprised at how what I wrote almost ten years ago is still highly relevant to the dynamics of the Slow Food international movement and to the world of gastronomy as a whole, yet still remains unaccomplished. I see how and how much some of the urgencies expressed in the book are still important for the achievement of a form of liberation that is easier to identify today, but is still relatively unacknowledged by those who do not march under the banner of the Slow Food snail.

Slow Food still needs to take a few decisive steps forward. Sometimes we lose sight of our main aims and fail to do enough to valorize the biological and human diversity that provides creative drive and energy to the network that we currently represent. And for the network that we are becoming: the network of Terra Madre, which, as it grows year by year, we are seeking to drive but not bridle under Slow Food control. In fact, we want Slow Food to be *in* the network, not *over* the network, in which case it would be outside it. We are also pondering whether the associational approach, a typically Western phenomenon that does not exist in many cultures round the world, is still valid. This is a question I shall return to later in the book but, in the meantime, it is an interesting exercise to assess the impact of "good, clean, and fair," partly because it provides an opportunity to stress how certain processes that have taken place in less complex gastronomic areas are not all that spontaneous and have yet to generate the steps hoped for toward some form of liberation.

But let us return to 2005. In the conclusions to the book I wrote:

I am a gastronome.

No, not a glutton with no sense of restraint whose enjoyment of food is greater the more plentiful and forbidden it is.

No, not a fool who is given to the pleasures of the table and indifferent to how the food got there.

I like to know the history of a food and of the place that it comes from; I like to imagine the hands of the people who grew it, transported it, processed it, and cooked it before it was served to me.

I do not want the food I consume to deprive others in the world of food.

I like traditional farmers, the relationship they have with the earth and the way they appreciate it was good.

The good belongs to everyone; pleasure belongs to everyone, for it is in human nature.

There is food for everyone on this planet, but not everyone eats. Those who do eat often do not enjoy it, but simply put gasoline into an engine. Those who do enjoy it often do not care about anything else: about the farmers and the earth, about nature and the food things it can offer us.

Few people know about the food they eat and derive enjoyment from that knowledge, a source of pleasure which unites all the people who share it.

I am a gastronome, and if that makes you smile, I assure you that it is not easy to be one. It is a complex matter, for gastronomy, though a Cinderella in the world of knowledge, is in fact a true science, which can open eyes.

And in the world of today it is very difficult to eat well, as gastronomy commands.

But there is a future even now, if the gastronome hungers for change.

In this "spontaneous declaration" at the end of the last chapter in the book, I argued that gastronomy is the science of happiness. I have to admit that some of my old gastronome friends were almost offended by the first sentences and some leveled barbed criticisms at me. It was only years later that they were eventually won over by "produce cooking" and the "new localism" in gastronomy now, fortunately, all the rage in the world's trendiest, and finest, restaurants. I have always maintained that the "good, clean, and fair" formula is not a dogma but an aspiration that traditional farmers, cooks, producers, and citizens should work toward—a triptych on which they can build an alliance. Over the last ten years, traveling through some of the least hospitable, forgotten areas of Italy, the world's urban peripheries, dry and wet zones, Africa, Central and South America with their new faces and old contradictions, the USA, the home of fast food, from west to east, I have come across many food products with all three characteristics.

I have the distinct sensation that a huge wave is swelling. Even the cooking of the great, most talked-about chefs—whose illustrious predecessors used to be convinced of the absolute supremacy of technique over primary ingredients, whatever they happened to be—is now based on select, strictly local food products and primary ingredients that are sustainable without any negative social implications. It is no coincidence that all this is happening in "virgin" territories, outside the boundaries of Eurocentric influence, where gastronomy has been rapidly liberated from the imprisoning stylistic features of the most classic French *grandeur gastronomique* to which we all owe so much— arguably everything in the early days. Yet this grandeur has also been questioned in France itself, where a period of grave crisis in the sector has led to more affordable, well-contextualized forms of catering alert to the world of agricultural production. The neo-bistro phenomenon is a case in point.

With time it is possible to better understand and valorize the various components of holistic, global gastronomic quality. We have liberated new energies from a sector that seemed to be asphyxiating, detached from reality, self-obsessed, blissfully deluded that it knew exactly what pleasure was. But it did not know at all. The fact that gastronomy involves much more than this broadens the field of action and multiplies pleasure in responsibility and in opportunities for worlds and people to meet.

- Good: attention to sensory quality, to pleasure (personal or shared, convivial), to taste, seen also in cultural terms (what is good for me may not be good in Africa, South America, in the Far East, and vice versa)

- Clean: the sustainability and durability of all food-related processes, from sowing with respect for biodiversity through cultivation to harvesting, from processing to transport, from distribution to end consumption, without waste, and based on conscious choices

- Fair: without exploitation, direct or indirect, of those who work in the countryside, with gratifying and adequate remuneration, with respect for buyers' pockets, valorizing equity, solidarity, donation, and sharing

This set of values is of great relevance today. There are those who have specialized in promoting or defending these values, even if only in part, but few grasp the importance of the set as a whole and the precious connections it hides. Our vision, instead, is holistic, all-inclusive, and complex. It is impossible to view food from one point of view only, pursuing good, clean, or fair singly and separately. There were people who were obsessed with good and then moved on to clean; others were concerned only with fair or clean only to realize just how important good was.

Something is starting to move—as Edgar Morin said, "effectively everything has begun again"[6]—but there are still bits missing and some connections are no longer visible. The road is still long, albeit slightly less rocky than before.

[6] In his "In praise of metamorphosis," published in *Le Monde* and *La Stampa* on January 20, 2010, Edgar Morin described these processes, arguing that, "Everything has to start again, And effectively everything has begun again already without our knowing it."

# CHAPTER 6

# I LIKE IT!

On March 31, 2012, I was traveling through Africa with a group of people. We had driven the previous day from the capital, Nairobi, a buzzing city of contrasts, traffic, and humidity, to Nakuru, bound for the Rift Valley. On the way we had traveled through unforgettable scenery and our eyes had feasted on some of the most breathtaking spectacles on earth. One such was the view across the valley as far as the horizon from a scenic point on the road for Gigil. Still dazed by so much beauty, that morning we set out early from Nakuru for Lare to visit the Slow Food presidium there, set up to protect the cultivation of the local pumpkin. Lare is situated in the Njoro district near the mountain forest of Mau, the largest in East Africa. It sits on one of the Rift Valley plateaus in an area where, probably due to climate change, levels of rainfall have changed dramatically in the last few years, with dire consequences for the food security of the population. It was no coincidence that, in the period in which we visited, the local farmers had been waiting a month for the rains to come.

In those parts such a long delay immediately translates to hunger, and the consequences of the unpredictability of the weather are much more serious than the minor nuisances we complain about in Europe.

The Lare pumpkin, which adapts well to semi-arid conditions, is being protected because it is threatened by other more productive, non-native commercial varieties. It goes a long way because it is possible to eat both its fruits (which can also be processed into preserves, flour, and juices) and its leaves. It thus ensures relative food self-sufficiency in critical periods like the one I walked into. It ought to have been a period for sowing, but for the moment that was impossible. The villagers were preoccupied but that did not stop them from laying on a very warm welcome. We walked into the yards of two simple houses whose inside layout reminded me vaguely of the two-room place my grandmother lived in sixty years ago, on the ground floor in a typical Bra courtyard. At the center of these yards in Lare flew a flag with the Slow Food snail symbol, and we were welcomed by solemn speeches and demonstrations about the local agriculture and biodiversity. Walking in the fields round the village, they showed us how they work the presidium pumpkin, from the selection of the seeds, which are exchanged among the farmers of the community, to the milling of grated dried pumpkins to produce a tasty flour that can be consumed all year round. Pale green with white stripes and orange flesh, the pumpkins were traditionally wrapped in straw and kept in wells dug into the soil, but today they are stored in granaries. The presidium came into being in 2009 following research into the traditional foods of the Molo region carried out by Kenyan students at the University of Gastronomic Sciences in Pollenzo.[7] The project brings together

---

[7] A university in Pollenzo, on the outskirts of Bra, designed by Slow Food and founded by a group of private and public investors in 2004. See chapter 10 (page 60).

thirty producers, eight men and twenty-two women, who have formed an association to work together at every stage of production. As is only natural in a place where agriculture still represents a resource of primary importance, a decisive role is being played by women, the true protagonists of the presidium.

The novel feature of the project is that the women also run a small restaurant called Slow Food Hotel. Like all the "restaurants" in the area, it is tiny and very modest indeed. The food is cooked in large pots and pans over a fire in the open yard. Inside, two long tables with benches take up most of the space. The day I visited there were so many of us we could hardly move, and we had to squeeze in to make room for everyone. Knowing about health problems I had had in the past, some of my collaborators, Italians and Kenyans, were a little worried about the hygiene, which was not exactly up to European HACCP (Hazard Analysis and Critical Control Points) standards. But actually everything was clean enough, dignifiedly poor and perfect—it was just different. Partly because it was well past one o'clock and I was starting to feel a bit peckish, I chose to ignore the querying glances of my traveling companions. A never-ending procession began to come in from the yard outside: pans and trays brimming over with sauces and stews, and dishes made with pumpkin and its leaves, such as kimoto, which also includes potatoes and fava beans. They had used the pumpkin flour to make chapatis, which, out of a freak of history—the vast deployment of Indian workers on the building of the Kenya-Uganda railway and the immigration that ensued—has become Kenya's national bread. After came *madanzi*, ring-shaped loaves, also made with pumpkin flour, toasted and boiled pumpkin seeds, a porridge, fantastic pumpkin juice, then meats—lamb and veal—served with the most varied condiments. Judging on appearance alone, picky Europeans would have turned up their noses and classic gourmets would have been appalled by the "presentation." But my memory of that meal is as one of the best I ate in three weeks of travel.

I just couldn't help bursting out, "*A l'è bun! A mi susì 'em pias!*" (It's good! I like it!). I was speaking in Piedmontese, my dialect, which I revert to to convey strong, visceral feelings. I wanted to express all my appreciation to the cooks, who laughed and smiled, partly out of happiness and partly out of emotion. What does "good" mean after all? That meal—rich and tasty and a little strange—gave me gastronomic pleasure. It allowed me to discover new flavors and it sated my appetite. It was also part and parcel of the context—of the food these people cultivate and raise and eat—but it almost made me feel at home, a different home but just as welcoming. The meal was the product of ancient tradition and new syncretism, of the skilled hands of women who were wonderful cooks and wonderful human beings, and it combined lots of savvy with lots of savor.

After my morning visit, I understood these people's problems, their anxiety about the weather, their ways of doing things and of being together. The meal was conviviality, pleasure in sharing, domestic technique and gastronomic creativity. I reflected on how the finest recipes of our own regional tradition have the same characteristics: the common memory of hunger past and the knack of women for making a lot with a little. *A l'era propi bun!* It really was good.

When we came out of that dim room-cum-restaurant, where there had been praying but, above all, singing and laughter, where we had joked about our differences as a way of feeling closer together, the sky had gone very cloudy. The fact was a cause for relief and a cause for more smiling, which became more relaxed as we took a series of souvenir photographs. Those smiles and the flavors of Slow Food Hotel are now stamped in my memory and will never be erased. Especially when I think about what is good and what is not good, and when I think about what a "liberated gastronomy" can mean in places like Africa.

# CHAPTER 7

# CLEAN WINES

In the last few years, no attentive gastronomes or wine enthusiasts worth their salt can have ignored the phenomenon of so-called "natural wine," provided, that is, they weren't completely and passionately immersed in it already. In *Naked Wine* (Da Capo, Cambridge, MA, 2011), Alice Feiring defines it simply as "a wine produced on a terrain that has undergone no chemical treatments, adding nothing and taking nothing away."

Readers of restaurant reviews may have been tempted recently to take a trip to Paris to sample the amazing cooking of the city's neo-bistros, revisitations of the classic bistro model: easygoing places with tiny tables, informal service, and short and sharp menus that vary according to what is on sale at the morning's market, meaning fresh, seasonal, local, organic produce. At the stove you find former Michelin-starred chefs or youngsters who did their apprenticeships in the kitchens of great restaurants, the sous chefs of renowned chefs, no longer prepared to

work in their shadow and keen to break free from all the para-
phernalia and costs and constrictions involved in the running
of a haute cuisine establishment. A new generation of chefs is
putting its signature on these simple, youthful, exciting bistros,
where choice may be limited but where you can eat high-quality
food relatively cheaply, just as in a traditional Italian osteria and
with the same social buzz. The formula was invented in Paris
and is now conquering the rest of France. Traces of it are to be
detected in other countries, too: in the style of new trattorias in
Italy, for example, and in what used to be known as *bar a tapas*
in Spain. Parisian bistros like Le Baratin, Septime, Saturne, La
Gazzetta, Racines, Rino, Aux Deux Amis, Chatomat, Roseval, and
Le Chateaubriand (which has caused a sensation in recent years
by regularly appearing among the best fifty restaurants in the
world, even though it does have different characteristics from
all the others) mark one of the most significant ongoing trends
in international catering. After long dark years, this *nouvelle
vague* has restored France to the world spotlight, as—in order
of appearance—elBulli and Noma have since done for Spain and
Scandinavia respectively, and Gastón Acurio and Alex Atala are
now doing for Latin America.

Another common thread that runs through all the neo-bistros
is the presence on almost every table of natural wines, served by
the bottle or by the glass: organic and biodynamic wines bereft
of sulfur dioxide, as unadulterated as possible, so that, according to producers and drinkers alike, they express the geographical context they come from more directly. Nature's revenge over
culture, one might say. The incredible boom of natural wine, now
tantamount to a fashion trend, has reached overinflated levels of
intensity and *terroirisme*, marked by heated debate between traditionalists and the champions of absolute cleanness. But we've
seen it all before.

In the way it has led to the formation of something similar to
parties and factions in the wine world, the natural wine debate is

reminiscent of the events that took place in Italy after the advent of barriques, or wood casks. It was precisely the generation of post-methanol youngsters, who had studied how great wines are aged in France, who introduced them. Barolo, Barbaresco, the so-called Super Tuscans, and many other of Italy's most tannic, potent wines drew benefits from the new canteen technique, sometimes achieving sensational results. Others smacked too much of wood, which was used to cover their defects. Sampling those wines, some tasters in Piedmont remarked that "*A smia 'd mordi 'na barrique*" (it's like biting into a barrique). Like everything else, winemaking is a matter of common sense and compromise, exalted by skill in the vineyard, technique in the cellar, and sensitivity for a continuously evolving living matter such as wine. The barrique helped many small Italian producers reach the international stage, hence the definition "international taste" for French, Italian, American, and Australian barrel-aged wines. I have no hesitation in admitting that I was enthusiastic about these wines, as were the tasters of the *Italian Wines* guide, which was then starting to orient the market with the annual assignment of its "Three Glasses" symbols.

The much-coveted symbols were showered on "barriqued" wines and this is maybe what induced so many producers to go down the new route. Those first few years marked a veritable renaissance in Italian winemaking, with many products improving in quality, starting to last longer and evolve better in the bottle, and ultimately managing to compete with the best crus of Burgundy and Bordeaux. As I said at the start of the chapter, it was a liberation. The success of the new production method led many to adopt it, but also to misuse it. So much so that, right from the outset, the great Barolo purists, such as Bartolo Mascarello (whose hand-drawn "No barrique—No Berlusconi" label, withdrawn from shop windows in Alba before a general election, has become the stuff of legend) and Battista Rinaldi, opposed the use of barriques, thereby demonstrating, among other things, that it was possible to make exceptional Barolo with the most traditional techniques and without the use of wood. The controversy looked as if it would drag on forever and, albeit with less clamor than then, still divides many enthusiasts. The difference is that today the debate is all about tastes and preferences and is no longer an almost "ideological" face-off.

At a certain point, barriques became fashionable. And like all fashions, once it had radically perverted its founding principles in order to follow the market, it seriously risked losing any of the value it might have had. At least judging from the wine lists and blackboards in Paris and from the choices of the many Italian restaurateurs who devote special attention to wine, today the fashion would appear to be natural wine. What is certain is that natural wine has fostered a minor revolution: by placing the emphasis on more eco- and health-conscious production processes; by liberating new denominations and terroirs and helping them to express their diversity; by driving critics out to "tour the vineyards" once more in order to get a better handle on the phenomenon. Judging from these products alone, the wine world seems to be enjoying a new renaissance, a new ferment, a new passion. Yet, while it is true that there are great wines among the natural ones (some are already historic, biodynamics having been adopted in some of the best Burgundy and Champagne crus for many years), but there are also phonies whose only claim to fame is that they are made strictly according to the rules of naturalness. The alleged rivalry between natural wines and the rest of wine production should be seen through the lens of the above considerations. More importantly, it poses philosophical questions about the very concepts of *naturalness* and *authenticity*. As Nicola Perullo wrote in an article published in the first 2013 issue of the Slow Food magazine *Slow*, in which he compared wine, a living being, to the human organism:

The question is complex and its boundaries are blurred. For example, dental care today is not considered a superfluous prosthesis like the injection of botulin into the lips, and the well-cared for teeth of a human being are not subjected to aesthetic disquisitions about the *naturalness* of a nice face in the way the use of Botox is. Something similar happens with wine: the use of sulfur dioxide is tolerated and accepted even by those who have a non-interventionist philosophy, and even biodynamics protocols envisage its use, albeit in very limited quantities compared to wines made with conventional procedures. The use, instead, of selected yeasts or of concentrators for fermentation or of liquid tannins or of additional aromas is much debated, criticized, and questioned. A certain wine ideology led us to believe that these differences were unimportant, as if we shouldn't care less about the difference between a body shaped by aesthetic surgery and one shaped without. The paradigm of standard "conventional" tasting has almost completely neglected (sometimes deliberately, more often that not out of blissful ignorance) recognition of these aspects [ . . . ] It is possible that, with respect to a code of authenticity based on previous cases, a certain natural wine may appear eccentric, off kilter. Each specific case thus has to be evaluated and each judgment mediated. If extreme positions exist to promote a philosophy of truly minimalist winemaking—without adding anything to the spontaneous processes of fermentation and maturation and accepting everything that follows—nonetheless most people prefer a minimally interventionist philosophy, adding as little as possible so that wine can always express itself at its best and follow its natural course, but correcting any "grave" defects. There are no aprioristic recipes or rules for this. To recognize authenticity and naturalness means to validate through attentive, sensitive drinking, a complex set of elements and recognizing them as a complex organism. The onus of proof of authenticity and naturalness lies with the expert wine lover. An aesthetic taste education is a compulsory horizon for natural wine.

The natural wine question, finally, has more to do with "good" than with anything else. It is bound up in taste and the last word belongs, in any case, to the attentive drinker, who makes his choices according to his own sensitivity and experience. Yet what interests me most about natural wines is the "clean" factor.

I see the Langa hills where I was born and I am reminded of the words of Bartolo Mascarello who, at the moment of greatest splendor for local winegrowers, argued that, "At the entrance to villages round here they should put up signs saying, 'Territory hit by sudden well-being'"—and he wasn't wrong. At a certain point, when people were starting earning a fortune with wine, horrendous warehouses began to proliferate in the Langa area, not only on the valley floor but also higher up, in the hills themselves. They didn't think twice about disemboweling entire hillsides to build newer, larger cellars beneath them. Sprawling new residences sprang up that to define as Hollywoodesque would be a compliment. Vineyards were often planted in poor locations and sometimes they stretched almost into the *bisun*, or irrigation channels. The sole aim was to boost production without a care for quality, to exploit the new golden goose producers—the hunger of their fathers still fresh in their memories—had stumbled across with their barrique-aged wines of exceptional quality, which were selling like hotcakes on overseas markets. In all these vineyards, they practiced carpet weed control with a generous use of chemical treatments, so much so that one producer confessed to me that he had moved over to organics because he was fed up of having to lock his children, who were showing clear signs of illness, in the house on days when the vines were being sprayed with plant protection products and pesticides. As the new vineyards appeared, so woodland disappeared, along with the hedgerows, which in the least favorable locations ensured the presence of small fauna and birds that fed on insects and parasites. A delicate balance was being broken and the soil was losing its fertility. These phenomena haven't disappeared altogether; the landscape is still being ravaged for the sake of profit and no care is given to the sustainability of processes. Barolo is very good, but is it "clean"? I have seen the once distinctive features of an entire local area—and of many people—change completely as a result of the sudden well-being denounced by Mascarello, and I'm convinced something has been lost in the process. This is certainly the case of beauty, but also of ecology, hence of productive potential in relation to the quality of wine.

So natural wines in general may not be the best in the world— though I am coming across more and more exceptional bottles— but I cannot help viewing them with affection; first because they are saving whole portions of vineyard and land from pollution and impoverishment; second because their producers hold the environment that surrounds them obsessively close to their hearts. With natural wines it is possible to preserve a great deal and to offer new possibilities to many native grape varieties, much to the benefit of biodiversity. Their productive process, moreover, is more respectful of nature and human health (suffice it to remember that methanol was once a permitted additive). All this can do no harm, and if self-discipline generates improved techniques, greater care, innovation, and, finally, great results, we cannot help feeling happy and liberated in the name of "clean"—and also of "good."

# CHAPTER 8
# SLAVES

Saluzzo is a historic town, in the province of Cuneo, which for the last forty years or so has been the main center of fruit-growing in Piedmont. In recent years, from June to October, it has been easy to note, out and about, how the town's population suddenly increases thanks to the arrival of hordes of foreigners, especially from Central Africa, though in the past there used to be no lack of Moroccans, Algerians, Albanians, and Poles, either. These men are farm laborers who come to pick the fruit in the surrounding countryside. If you drive through the area, you will be amazed by the expanses of orchards you travel past. In 2012, about four hundred migrants came to Saluzzo, but the number is increasing every year. Four hundred new people in a town with a population of 17,000 do not go unnoticed, but here they are treated relatively well compared to other places in Italy, and we shall soon see why. Yet though, with no help from the Provincial and Regional Authorities, the Municipality of Saluzzo has made clean, well-appointed living facilities available, there are not enough of them. The only solution for people flocking in from situations of extreme poverty in search of fortune is to camp out. Hence makeshift campsites spring up that—as happened in June 2013—the police are subsequently forced to dismantle. And it is thus that the whole town is forced to ask itself whether this is fair or not, to ask questions about the meaning of the word "welcome," and to risk being the butt of glib accusations of racism. It is a huge problem and the inhabitants address it as best they can.

Saluzzo is used to these pacific invasions. Vast orchards have been growing around the town for half a century and the need for labor in the countryside did not crop up overnight. At one time, in the 1960s and 1970s, seasonal workers used to arrive en masse from the South of Italy, and until recently it was something of a tradition for local schoolchildren to pick fruit to earn themselves a few lire for their summer vacations. Today even in the South of Italy the locals do not pick fruit anymore; there, too, the job is left to foreigners, often illegal immigrants. In Saluzzo itself, high school students would no longer dream of going to work in the fields in the summertime.

In a delicate situation like that of Saluzzo, a campsite inhabited by people with no concrete job prospects (in 2013, the harvesting season was late in coming), in which the living conditions are unacceptable, becomes an easy target, a chance for easy pickings for aspiring *caporali*, illegal recruiters of farm laborers, and other wheeler-dealers. The people living there become a target for blackmail and they are liable, out of mere necessity, to opt for a life of crime and the mirage of an income.

Illegality reigns supreme in the Italian countryside, as if it, too, were a "seasonal product." According to FLAI-CGIL, the national federation of agro-industrial workers, a trade union very sensitive to the question, 400,000 farm workers are illegally recruited in Italy every year, 60,000 of them living in utter squalor in houses without the minimum requisites of fitness for habitation. The recruiters are ruthless types and are part of a phenomenon that is rife in other sectors, too, most notably the building trade. Today they are no longer all Italians, some of them being Africans like the exploited workers themselves; hence a war among the poor in which mafia infiltrations are not uncommon. Entrepreneurs entrust recruiters with the power to run the lives of workers in fields far away from the urban centers. What the eye can't see, the heart doesn't grieve over; far less can anyone demand regularity and legality. Everything is off the book: it has been estimated that moonlighting accounts for 90 percent of all agricultural labor in the South of Italy, for 50 percent in the Center, and for 30 percent in the North. The problem is not one of seeing that contracts are respected, it is that these workers don't even "exist."

They are as "seasonal" as the fruit and vegetables they pick, and they travel all around the country. In July and August, they concentrate in Puglia, especially in the Capitanata district in the province of Foggia or on the Salentine Peninsula, the heel of the Italian boot. Then they make straight for the Palazzo San Gervasio area in Basilicata, where the tomatoes are harvested later in the season. They are to be found in Campania, at Piana del Sele, in the province of Salerno, at Villa Literno, and Castel Volturno in the province of Caserta. In the autumn and winter, they turn up in Calabria at Rosarno on the Piana di Gioia Tauro plain, in Sicily, where illegal recruiting goes on everywhere until the spring, when potatoes and other vegetables are harvested. The phenomenon also appears in the North of Italy: in Piedmont, round Modena and Cesena in Emilia Romagna in the fruit-picking season, in Padua in Veneto, in Mantua in Lombardy for the melon harvest, and even in the civilized Trentino–Alto Adige region for the apple harvest. It is a recurring problem but we only ever hear about it in the most sensational cases.

One example still fresh in the memory is the revolt in Rosarno, in Calabria, during the citrus fruit harvest in January 2010. There an incident in which unidentified individuals shot at a group of migrants on their way back from the fields with an air pistol was followed by two days of clashes. Then a protest march by 2,000 workers led to three-way face-offs involving the police, the workers, and the locals. The final casualty list spoke of fifty-three people wounded or injured, a couple of whom very seriously so. In subsequent revenge missions, some of the immigrants were shot in the legs and a shed they were sleeping in was set on fire.

In July 2011, the event that provoked most scandal was a strike in Nardò, in Puglia. A year later, I interviewed one of the leaders of the protest—which led to the arrest of landowners and recruiters—for "*Storie di Piemonte*" (Stories from Piedmont), the weekly column I write in the regional pages of the daily newspaper *La Repubblica*. Yvan Sagnet is a young man from Cameroon who came to Turin in 2007 to study Telecommunications Engineering, and four years later ended up living a nightmare. The following extract from the interview gives some idea of what the illegal recruitment of farm laborers entails:

"In the summer of 2011 I discovered I had lost my scholarship," says Yvan. "It was harder to find work. I needed to earn more money, so I followed a friend's advice and set off for Puglia to pick tomatoes and watermelons. In Nardò they put me up in a farmhouse that belonged to the municipality. It had been converted into a reception center for immigrants and local voluntary associations were trying to make life easier for field workers there. It was like a little African township with casual commercial dealings and far more people than it had room for. I had to buy a mattress for five euros but it got stolen immediately. To have a shower in appalling hygienic condition you had to queue up for hours. The impact was very traumatic. Then the recruiters came to give us work [ . . . ] First they picked out the people with their documents in order like myself, then they took them off us. It was only later that I figured out they were using them to cover up for the work of people without residence permits who are paid 2.50 euros per crate of tomatoes against 3.50 for the regular workers. After ten days' waiting, at last they gave me my documents back and I started working." His recruiters were Sudanese; they used to come to pick the workers up at 4 o'clock in the morning to take them to the fields and made them pay 5 euros for transport. The workers had to work from 14 to 16 hours in succession, out in the sun at a temperature of 40°C, and were forced to travel from the farmhouse to the fields packed inside a covered van whose windows were blacked over. They had to pay 3.50 euros for a sandwich and 1.50 for a bottle of water and they couldn't take anything with them from the farmhouse. "The first day of work, I felt I'd reached rock-bottom. I filled only four 500 kilo crates and I was a psychological wreck. The others were more experienced than I was and could manage 15, maybe even 20 crates. So I dug in my heels and I decided to do better. I managed to get up to an average of eight crates a day, scrimping and saving just a little cash, net of expenses. [*Author's Note:* Doing the math, eight crates equals 28 euros, less a sandwich, a bottle of water or two, and 10 euros to go back and forth from the farmhouse, so Yvan was earning less than a euro an hour for 15 hours' work.] After four days' living like that, Yvan was asked to work even harder. He and some others decided to drop tools and brandish what should have been their legal labor agreement and envisaged totally different conditions. The protest spread to the farmhouse in what was to be remembered as the Nardò strike. The workers managed to obtain better conditions and, above all, the matter became public knowledge and proved decisive for the passing of an anti-recruiting law that had been lying idle in Parliament for some time.

Today Yvan is happy and well, has a degree, and works as a trade union leader. He has appeared on television and been much written about. All's well that ends well, but Yvan's is also a cautionary tale that reminds us that, despite harsher laws, the phenomenon of illegal recruitment continues. Just as they turn up in Saluzzo, so migrant workers turn up elsewhere. They are hungry and all they want is a job, but sometimes they sink into horrifying situations that, in many cases, are passed over in silence. A few years ago, an investigation by the Italian weekly magazine *L'Espresso* told of people dying of fatigue and, since they had neither names nor documents, being buried any old how.

Unfortunately, our consumption of fruit and vegetables may be partly to blame for the scandal. It is virtually impossible to be sure whether a tomato, say, or a melon, a watermelon, an orange, or a clementine has passed through these people's desperate hands. If we were sure, no one would buy them. These workers are not free, and neither are we. This, alas, is part of gastronomy, too, another sense in which it still needs to be liberated. "Good" and "Clean" may be easy to understand, partly because great progress has been made on these two counts, but the "Fair" element in the triptych is arguably harder to grasp. Now you may appreciate what it means. And you may also appreciate that there is still a great deal of work to be done, in Italy and in the rest of the world, where the rights of millions of field workers and smallholders and peasants are still not respected.

# CHAPTER 9
# UNISG

In 1998, I managed at last to enter a place that had been firing my curiosity for decades. Every time I walked across the small central piazza in Pollenzo, a tiny village of Roman origin just outside Bra, I used to wonder what lay behind the long railings grown over with ivy and weeds and brambles opposite the parish church, built in a bizarre neo-Gothic style in the mid-nineteenth century. The council had set up huge metal panels in front of the railings to stick up propaganda at election time and advertising posters for the rest of the year, but behind them one could make out a large building with two turrets in the private portion of what had once been a great Savoy family estate. It was not far from the castle, which was also closed to the public. For years, ever since the property had been sold to a family of former industrialists, nobody had been allowed in. I was very curious to find out more about the place. I then heard that the huge property, excluding the castle, had been put up for sale.

That was a good reason in itself for going to have a look round at last.

The Agenzia di Pollenzo (that is the name of the place), together with the church, the portico around the piazza, an odd-looking crenellated tower, and the castle, was built in the first half of the nineteenth century by Carlo Alberto of Savoy. It was a large, indeed enormous, royal farm, neo-Gothic outside and neoclassic inside with a square ground plan. The first time I saw it inside, it was in a sorry state. Originally built by the Savoys to house the administrative and estate management offices and provide a warehouse for the grain and agricultural produce from the vast royal lands, it had been used as a barn and as a storehouse for agricultural utensils. It also housed a huge wine cellar where, I was to find out later, a certain General Staglieno, a wine enthusiast, had carried out his first experiments to make Barolo more cellarable, capable of competing with the French wines that were drunk at court. The Agenzia was one of the hubs of the farming activity of the Piedmontese and, subsequently, the Italian royals. In 1998, albeit in a state of neglect, it was still serving its purpose, at least in part: as a storehouse for agricultural produce and utensils, as an aviary for breeding pheasants, which were then released in the surrounding reserve in the hunting season, as a breeding farm for poultry and rabbits. The building, very beautiful and very grand, was falling to bits and it was going to cost a fortune to repair it.

Half jokingly, I took Giovanni Ravinale, a friend who was like a brother to me, with me on that first visit. He looked at me as if I was mad. He couldn't figure out whether this was just another of the practical jokes we used to play on each other or organized together for a laugh, or whether I—without a penny in my pocket, incidentally—really was thinking about buying that gigantic ruin. When I saw the immense 1,700-square-meter cellar, my thoughts strayed immediately to the great *courtiers* of France, the middlemen who traditionally buy cellarable wines when they are young, stock them in châteaux, and sell them off in the fullness of time. The tradition goes back a long way in France's best wine-growing areas, where it has led to the setting up of veritable wine banks. These not only allow one to buy wine virtually of any vintage, but also preserve the historical memory of their own local wines, even the very oldest. Here it is possible to make comparative tastings of the most disparate vintages, a practice that has done much to create and maintain the myth of wines such as Bordeaux and Burgundy. In 1998, in the Langa area, on the other hand, one struggled to find a Barolo or a Barbaresco from 1990, a fantastic vintage, just five years after their release. Bottles had sold like hotcakes at very high prices—and rightly so—but there were none left to hand down to prosperity. We might never have known how those important wines would evolve over the decades to follow. The emotion of uncorking a French *premier cru* a hundred years after bottling and discovering it was still a great wine would not have been repeatable with great Langa wines. "Here we'll have a wine bank as a historical memory of our terroir," I told Giovanni. "We've got to get producers involved in the adventure immediately." So we spoke about it with our regular collaborators at Slow Food—in those days there were no more than about thirty of us working in the offices—and embarked on an adventure that seemed far too big for us, but which is now rewarding us with enormous satisfactions. The project was a fundamental achievement in the process of the liberation of gastronomy. It gave the theory of the complexity of gastronomic science and "Good" and "Clean" and "Fair" walls to live between, to grow between, to evolve between—a place where they could be studied.

Giovanni Ravinale embodied the first "office" dedicated to the forming of a joint-stock company—subsequently a public company thanks to the intervention of the institutions—to raise the money needed for the investment. It was with great determination that we set out to do the rounds of all the people who might be interested to rope them into the Wine Bank project, top of the list being the Langa wine producers. Things went well and in three years we managed to buy the property, and in another three to totally restructure it. Then we began thinking about how to fill the quadrilateral of very spacious buildings that stood above the cellars. If the developing of a hotel and restaurant with international appeal was a pretty obvious choice—hence the Albergo dell'Agenzia and Ristorante Guido, now converted into a students' restaurant—that of founding a full-fledged university was less so: a University of Gastronomic Sciences, the UNISG as we call it today.

Slow Food had been involved in food and taste education for some time. Taste Workshops were enjoying increasing success in the various events we organized: the Salone del Gusto first and foremost, but also Cheese, Slow Fish, and smaller regional gatherings. As we have seen, the Workshops had a precise format, but this soon evolved to become less tied to the events themselves and no longer directed only at adults. This is why we launched the Masters of Food, evening courses about the various food product categories organized in Slow Food convivia all over Italy—something akin to a popular university—plus a whole range of initiatives with schoolteachers. We also set up an Education Office, which now runs a School Garden project for small children at a local level and training programs in state schools. As our commitment gradually grew, we increasingly felt the need for the academic world to engage with gastronomy and study it as a real science. *Buono, pulito e giusto* was published in 2005, but the idea for a University or Academy of Taste had already taken root in 2000. We planned to house it in the buildings of the Agenzia di Pollenzo, which were then in the process of being restructured. In those days, we were already convinced that gastronomy was a complex, multidisciplinary subject and everything we were working on was moving in that direction. I will not speak at length about the endless difficulties we had to address—and which still pop up from time to time—in chipping away at the Italian academic empire to make it accept a new subject that was not envisaged in the official syllabuses of the Ministry of Education and Research. Nor do I want to describe all the obstacles the mandarins of the academic world laid in our way. It would take a whole book to explain how closed and narrow that world is, how enlightened minds are conspicuous by their absence there, how the majority of its inhabitants are virtually incapable of overriding barriers among the various disciplines and specializations—which, after all, represent their own little realms of knowledge. It was one of the hardest battles we at Slow Food have ever had to fight, but in the end we won thanks to a stubbornness born of iron conviction in our own ideas.

In 2004, together with the newly restructured Wine Bank, the Albergo dell'Agenzia, and Ristorante Guido,[8] we inaugurated the University of Gastronomic Sciences, which welcomed its first seventy-five students, most of whom were from abroad. We had created a new subject for university study, we had endowed gastronomy with academic dignity. Another fundamental step forward toward a liberated gastronomy. Unfortunately, my friend Giovanni was no longer with us on the day of the inauguration, having passed away suddenly in 1999, just a year after work on the rebuilding of the Agenzia di Pollenzo had begun. He was the first person to believe in the project, so it is only normal, when I think about that period, about the crazy idea of raising millions of euros for that Utopian enterprise, for me to think about him, too.

---

[8] The Banco del Vino, Wine Bank, an archive-cum-museum of fine Italian wines, housed in the estate's nineteenth-century cellars, the Albergo dell' Agenzia, a four-star hotel with restaurant, and Ristorante Guido, a Michelin-starred restaurant serving traditional Piedmontese fare (now closed).

Then I think how certain passions are a little like friendship: they know no boundaries, they know no obstacles. They are ideas, they are feelings, they are something to believe in. If you sow your seeds well, Utopia allows you to harvest reality. This is what we are continuing to do, even as our group of friends around the world enjoying the fruits of liberated gastronomy grows out of all proportion.

# CHAPTER 10

# WHAT A SCIENCE!

Today the University of Gastronomic Sciences' website explains its mission as follows:

Its goal is to create an international research and education center for those working on renewing farming methods, protecting biodiversity, and building an organic relationship between gastronomy and agricultural science. The result is a new professional figure—the gastronome—skilled in production, distribution, promotion, and communication of high-quality foods. Gastronomes are the next generation of educators and innovators, editors and multimedia broadcasters, marketers of fine products, and managers of consortia, businesses, and tourism companies. UNISG students, hailing from around the world, gain dynamic experiences in artisanal and industrial food production, thanks to complementary education in both science and humanities, sensory training, and hands-on learning during study trips (field seminars) across five

continents. To date, more than 1,000 students have studied or are studying at UNISG.

Imagine the scene when we got round the table to decide
exactly what a gastronome ought to study. It was 2002–2003
and we would often meet in Verduno,[9] at the Real Castello, an
excellent hotel-restaurant of sober charm, rich in history, which
Nuto Revelli[10] adopted as his *buen retiro* in the last summers of
his life. There, he and I would have long, inspirational conver-
sations about the farming culture of our local area, about the
value of memory, about the importance of recording the wisdom
and memories of our elders. I had summoned all my finest collaborators, among whom was Professor Alberto Capatti, later to
become the first dean of the University, a historian of French
gastronomy and former editor of the avant-garde gastronomic
review *La Gola*, "a monthly of food and material life techniques,"
which taught us all a lot from 1982 to 1988. The first working group that got together at Verduno also included Massimo
Montanari, Marco Riva, and Fausto Cantarelli.[11] In those early
meetings, we tried to fit our new subject, gastronomic science,
into the ministerial schedules, to make the idea we had in mind
match the red tape. The combination of certain subjects together
on the same course was not contemplated in Italian universities:
sociology did not go very well with biology, agriculture was not
part of the curriculum of people studying the psychology of cog-

---

[9] Small hilltop village with an eighteenth-century Savoy royal castle, a few
miles from Bra and Pollenzo.

[10] Benvenuto "Nuto" Revelli (1919–2004), Italian military officer, partisan,
and writer, famous for his books on the resistance during World War II and on
rural conditions and emigration in the postwar years.

[11] Massimo Montanari (1949–), professor of Medieval History at the University
of Bologna; Marco Riva (1951–2008), food technologist and writer; Fausto
Cantarelli (1932–), economist specializing in food and agriculture.

nitive processes. We also needed to introduce new subjects, such as the history of gastronomy and sensory analysis. Last but not least, we had to officialize one of the best ways a gastronome has to learn, the one my generation and I, all of us self-taught, used to learn: namely travel and firsthand knowledge, "touring the country" and the places where food is produced.

In our meetings we began to put down in writing a program of study periods that students still follow, setting out on journeys that take them round Italy and abroad as part of their syllabus. They go to Africa to see what communities cultivate and cook, they travel every inch of the Italian countryside, they visit the largest and best food companies (yes, some of these actually do a good job), they stay for a couple of days, say, with Italian and international presidium producers, they go to find out more about Asian or South American cooking traditions, they explore the latest trends in the restaurant industry and food distribution. Study trips, which involve groups of about ten students, are conducted by dedicated tutors, often assisted or guided by Slow Food collaborators, and they exploit the Slow Food and Terra Madre international network. They are an element of some importance for the diffusion and sharing of the precepts of the new gastronomic science as we conceived it, and are also a novel feature on the Italian university scene.

Once home from their trips, students use the audiovisual material they have collected and the notes they have taken to prepare a presentation to share what they have seen and learned with their colleagues, who have made different trips to different places. It is a sort of "competition" in which a jury of members of the teaching staff assigns marks, which count as credits for the students' degrees. Study trips are important as a more direct way of lending academic dignity to the old skills of farmers, food artisans and producers, livestock breeders, and sustainable food distributors, turning the latter, too, into "teachers"—a role that befits them. The trips realize the "dialogue between realms" that I have been preaching for at least ten years, attempting to persuade official and academic science to put itself on the same plane as the traditional wisdom of the food world and establishing a level playing field of dialectics and interaction.

The annual study trip program on its own makes the UNISG unique. But it is also unique for the way in which it has succeeded in creating a curriculum scientifically inspired by all the possible nuances of "good, clean, and fair," tying in distinct skills and disciplines, organizing innovative fields of research, asserting itself as a center of excellence for the study of a subject that was born inside an association and grew up in the world at large. The only mistake we made was not to include ecology as a subject for study right at the beginning, but since then we have remedied this by introducing the systemic paradigm based on the theories of Fritjof Capra.[12] Liberated gastronomy now has a university of its own, which promises to take the science further, enabling it to break free from the trap set by the fanatics who give marks to restaurants and bottles of wine, to evade the dumbing-down of a subject as noble and precious as food that we witness on our television screens, to escape the elite world of bon vivants who make no effort to assume responsibility for their surroundings. The university, moreover, can offer future prospects for young people by transforming itself into a place of study and exchange, a place to explore uncharted territories of knowledge, a place for designing new paradigms useful not only among the groves of academe.

I believe that the University of Gastronomic Sciences project, together with Terra Madre, is the jewel in the Slow Food crown, that it has generated all the progress the movement has made since.

---

[12] Fritjof Capra (1939–), Austrian physicist and writer.

Far from being at an end, it is now being enriched by new perspectives. Perhaps people have yet to fully understand how precious the youngsters who graduate from Pollenzo are, how important it is for the professors and lecturers to live and breathe the air of this university. What they certainly do not understand yet is that setting up a university dedicated to "Good, Clean, and Fair" was not a megalomaniac exercise in vanity and egocentrism. Today we have before us an international think tank (half the students come from abroad, from every continent in the world), where a new form of knowledge is being learned and transmitted. A new way of seeing food is being born that takes in all its implications, even the most unlikely, a holistic vision that places all subjects on an equal footing, without discrimination. The degree theses of students at Pollenzo are becoming an important baggage for the Slow Food network and anyone drawn to the new gastronomic science. I would even go so far to say that the UNISG is becoming a sort of Frankfurt School of gastronomy. Thanks to the project we sketched out in the rooms of Verduno castle, a new, accredited category of knowledge has been created that now enables many other universities, at last recognized by the state (an achievement in itself!), to activate their own courses of gastronomic sciences. Yet the Pollenzo approach remains inimitable because, in Pollenzo, we do not work with the knowledge categories many academics are accustomed to. Instead, we attach equal importance to so-called "noble" learning and to popular, sometimes unwritten learning, attributing unprecedented importance to orality, not just in an anthropological sense.

The UNISG is looked down upon by those who still think food is a frivolous subject (many university professors in Italy and overseas are still under the impression that at Pollenzo we teach people how to cook!), but, in reality, it is a laboratory where food sustainability is studied scientifically, where the humanistic and technological approach combine as one, where history goes hand in hand with chemistry, ethnobotany with aesthetics, vegetable and animal food products with sensory analysis. At Pollenzo, students study the food network and we feed the network of those who want that food to be of absolute quality, respecting the criteria of the "good, clean, and fair" triptych coined by Slow Food. The food industry has not remained indifferent to all this and we have created a group of "strategic partners" with whom we work, with the world's future at heart, to create different forms of production and distribution.

It is wrong to dismiss an approach of this type as being muddled. A muddle is what is being created by people who attempt to do the same thing without the baggage of experiences and meetings and study that we have accumulated over the years. It is a baggage that would not exist without the revelations of the post-methanol period, without the Taste Workshops, without approaching all the "good people" in the world, without the "Clean" revolution, without social justice, without meeting and exchange—as open as possible—among areas and people that otherwise might never have come into contact.

A science has been born and defined. Maybe it is exact, maybe not, but what is certain is that, insofar as we never forget what pleasure means or where we set out from and why, it is a science at the service of happiness. We were in a trap but now we are free.

# CHAPTER II

# WHAT NEXT?

**W**hen they are freed, an animal that has always lived in a cage or a person who has been in prison for many years is bound to feel at least a bit disoriented. It is after liberation that the hard part comes: the animal has to learn to feed itself on its own and it won't necessarily survive (I have always been amused by the question Michael Pollan asks animalists. What would happen to hens set free from a henhouse? Answer: they would probably be killed by a fox or a pine marten), while the ex con would struggle to find a job, integrate into society, and overcome the prejudices that surround him. Sure, they would be free, but to do what?

Now that it has shaken off its yoke, gastronomy, too, is limping along uncertainly and paying the price of prejudice. It is not immune from contradictions, but these are actually a sign of complexity. We have freed gastronomy, but is it really free? The easy answer is no. You only have to switch on the television to see why. I have already evoked analogies with pornography. Food on TV is pure showbiz, with competitions between cooks that boil down to a race against the clock; recipes that have to be thrown together in a few minutes for the husband just home from work who wants to watch the news; restaurants that are madhouses in which chefs alternate excesses of rudeness and seductiveness; primary ingredients that are treated as unimportant; producers and farmers who are shown like animals at the zoo, to accentuate their curious, often bizarre sides. Often even the sternest critics of this TV ignorance fail to realize that all they have to counter it is an antiquated model of gastronomy that champions an elitist approach to the enjoyment of food: the restaurant as a holy place where the cult of personality surrounding chefs is defended to the hilt; recipes that are always sublime and superlative, not to mention photogenic; expensive, super-select primary ingredients. That of the classic old gourmet model of the connoisseur who invests himself with innate—more often than not impromptu—critical skills is a world in which the farmer does not exist. Gastronomic criticism has evolved with the web and now has more power than ever in terms of diffusion and capacity to reach an increasingly interested audience. Read through the right filters, it provides a service, but especially on the Internet, the range of a food writer rarely extends beyond restaurant reviews, personal takes on recipes, classifications of merit, a plug here and a snatch of gossip there. This is what attracts audiences on both television and computer screens, and this, too, is a response to food's worst enemy, the market. Rightly or wrongly, there is a lot of talk these days about Good, but the questions of Clean and Fair are either ignored or seen as a boring fixation on the part of "Slow Foodites," people who defend the past (hadn't we said that we intended to erase it and its backyard gastronomy?) and the environment, nitpickers who don't want us to eat tuna fish and salmon anymore? "Zero food miles" rhetoric, used at every turn in the most unlikely contexts without taking account of the fact that the local and the seasonal are a complex matter, is now devoid of content, like the environmentalist refrain of the 1980s. Some think that this is all we are; it's a matter of points of view.

I personally am happy to sit back and enjoy hearing everyone singing the praises of the cooks and chefs of the new wave of French bistros and the finest North and Latin American cuisine restaurants, all in search of good and clean food products that respect the dignity of farmers and often translate into direct collaborations and exchanges of products and knowledge. No wonder food bloggers now venture out of their usual circles of restaurateur and producer friends, who invite them to their own initiatives, and travel to Mexico, say, to discover the meaning of biodiversity in products that had previously all seemed the same and, amazed by so much wealth, advocate its protection; or when, on vacation they meet a peasant who changes their lives—or at least their way of seeing food—by letting them taste things they had never tasted before. Whether it is young people bridging a gap caused by inexperience or more seasoned journalists capable of taking new ideas on board, I am happy when I see this happen. I can sense that a network is growing and, above all, I convince myself that the role of small farmers and producers in local areas where gastronomy is not enslaved—simply because it has never existed there as we know it—will be a great driving force for change in the future. I can sense that gastronomy is being liberated thanks to their labor, to a mixture of different ways of seeing and doing things. I can sense that our past and our present, in which gastronomy was and is treated as little more than a game, reveal a model that we should not follow, but that will prove useful. Not only producers but also cooks and chefs are well ahead of the critics. In 2011, for example, some of the best chefs in the world met in Lima and wrote an "Open Letter to the Chefs of Tomorrow," later renamed the "Declaration of

Lima," that suggests we rethink the direction we are moving in and acknowledge that something has effectively changed over the last thirty years. Paolo Marchi was the first to speak about this in Italy in an article on *Identità golose*.[13] This is what he wrote:

Yesterday, Sunday, September 11, in Lima, in Peru, during the Mistura event [*Author's note:* which I shall return to later], the chefs who make up the International Consultancy Board of the Basque Culinary Center in San Sebastian, in the Basque Countries, the University of Gastronomic Sciences [*Author's note:* another one!] and its Center for Research and Innovation presented an "Open Letter to the Chefs of Tomorrow." I have translated it. One thing is for sure: years and years of Slow Food haven't passed by in vain in the four corners of the planet:

"At a time when society is rapidly changing, our profession must actively respond to new challenges. The culinary profession of today offers a wide variety of opportunities and trajectories. We chefs remain united by a passion for cooking and share the belief that our work is also a way of life. For us, cooking offers a world of possibilities, allowing us to freely express ourselves, pursue our interests, and fulfill our dreams. Indeed, we believe that cooking is not only a response to the basic human need of feeding ourselves; it is also more than the search for happiness. Cooking is a powerful, transformative tool that, through the joint effort of co-producers—whether we be chefs, producers or consumers—can change the way the world nourishes itself. We dream of a future in which the chef is socially engaged, conscious of and responsible for his or her contribution to a fair and sustainable society [ . . . ] To all of you, we direct this reflection, entitled 'An Open Letter to the Chefs of Tomorrow.'"

---

[13] Italian gastronomy website (www.identitagolose.it/sito/en/) founded in 2004.

There follow seven points, subdivided into four subjects: Nature (two), Society (two), Knowledge (two) and Values (one):

"Dear chef, in relation with nature:

1. Our work depends on nature's gifts. As a result we all have a responsibility to know and protect nature, to use our cooking and our voices as a tool for recovering heirloom and endangered varieties and species, and promoting new ones. In this way we can help protect the earth's biodiversity, as well as preserve and create flavors and to elaborate culinary methods.

2. Over the course of thousands of years, the dialogue between humans and nature has created agriculture. We are all, in other words, part of an ecological system. To ensure that this ecology is as healthy as possible, let's encourage and practice sustainable production in the field and in the kitchen. In this way, we can create authentic flavor.

In relation with society:

3. As chefs, we are the product of our culture. Each of us is heir to a legacy of flavors, dining customs, and cooking techniques. Yet we don't have to be passive. Through our cooking, our ethics, and our aesthetics, we can contribute to the culture and identity of a people, a region, a country. We can also serve as an important bridge with other cultures.

4. We practice a profession that has the power to affect the socioeconomic development of others. We can have a significant economic impact by encouraging the exportation of our own culinary culture and fomenting others' interest in it. At the same time, by collaborating with local producers and employing fair economic practices, we can generate sustainable local wealth and financially strengthen our communities.

In relation with knowledge:

5. Although a primary goal of our profession is to provide happiness and stir emotions, through our own work and by working with experts in the fields of health and education, we have a unique opportunity to transmit our knowledge to members of the public, helping them, for example, to acquire good cooking habits, and to learn to make healthy choices about the foods they eat.

6. Through our profession, we have the opportunity to generate new knowledge, whether it be something so simple as the development of a recipe or as complicated as an in-depth research project. And just as we have each benefited from the teaching of others, we have a responsibility, in turn, to share our learning.

In relation with values:

7. We live in a time in which cooking can be a beautiful form of self-expression. Cooking today is a field in constant evolution that includes many different disciplines. For that reason, it's important to carry out our quests and fulfill our dreams with authenticity, humility, and, above all, passion. Ultimately, we are each guided by our own ethics and values."

The document was signed by Ferran Adriá (elBulli, Spain), René Redzepi (Noma, Denmark), Alex Atala (D.O.M., Brazil), Massimo Bottura (Osteria Francescana, Italy), Gastón Acurio (Astrid y Gaston, Peru), Dan Barber (Blue Hill, USA), Michel Bras (Bras, France), Yukkio Hattori (Japan) and Heston Blumenthal (The Fat Duck, UK). [*Author's note:* Blumenthal subsequently denied signing the letter and had his signature removed.] The G9 of the restaurant industry.

What can I add? Gastronomy has been liberated itself and the phenomenon is now irreversible. Now it is up to us—food and wine critics, university lecturers, farmers, artisans, cooks, enthusiasts, citizens—to turn it into something that can change the world and walk tall without the uncertainty of someone who has just been released from captivity. It is up to us to use the energy released by the union of our diversities well. To make sure that food becomes the tool for a transformation so profound as to make our lives and those of future generations better and happier.

# II. LIBERATING DIVERSITY

## CHAPTER I

# IN SEARCH OF
# THE MISSIONARY

In 1983, I set off for a vacation in Brazil with a couple of friends from Bra. Our idea was to make a tour of a few cities and tourist locales, but the ultimate destination of our journey was Amazonia, which we planned to "explore," partly with the help of some missionaries from nearby Cuneo with whom we had indirect contacts. Bra is a small place and, before we left, word got around that we would be going to Manaus. Which is how we came to be approached by a lady who asked us to search for her son, a priest, Cravero by name, who had gone on a mission near the Amazonian city a few years earlier. Cravero's mother and brothers had heard nothing from him for months. In those pre-Internet and pre-satellite phone days, there was nothing strange about a missionary finding himself isolated in such remote areas, but Signora Cravero was very keen for us to deliver her son a food package and a letter as a way of being closer to him.

She was a very nice woman and we willingly agreed to help—though we weren't overjoyed at the prospect of carting a food parcel around Brazil with us. When, after various peregrinations, we eventually reached Manaus, the first thing we wanted to do was get rid of the parcel, which had become one of the running jokes of our vacation. After leaving our luggage at the hotel, we set off to look for the address Signora Cravero had given us. We were amazed to discover that the place wasn't there anymore. At that point we went to the Archbishop's palace to ask for news about our fellow citizen, but no one there had a clue who he was. They directed us to the Capuchin monastery, where all the monks were Italians. When we got there, about an hour later, we knocked on the door. It was opened by an elderly monk from Rieti[14] with a distinct regional accent.

"Cravero? I don't know who you're talking about," he said, looking a little startled. "Never heard of him before."

"Maybe he's on a mission? Maybe he's in some village somewhere?"

"No, we don't go out to the villages anymore. They don't listen to us. We say 'Ave Maria' and they think we're saying 'swollen river' in their language. A swollen river next to the Amazon! They just start laughing. They don't listen, it's all pointless. They've got their own rites and they're not going to change them. We're useless here."

In the meantime, the Guardian Father had walked up. Hearing his brother's pessimism, he gave him a good-natured telling off. "We aren't useless at all, we're here for the love of God."

"Love of God indeed, love of God! We're only wasting our time, we can't even catechize them. No, no, forget it, forget it. Let divine goodness and providence go with us!" said the monk who had opened the door.

---

[14] Small town in the Lazio region, in Central Italy.

"So what about our fellow citizen, Cravero?" I insisted.

"Try the Salesians," replied the two monks. "There are more of them than us."

So we set off for the Salesian school, still carrying Signora Cravero's food parcel with us. I hated to imagine what sort of state the food would be in after all that heat and all that traveling. The style of the father who welcomed us—he was wearing a polo-neck sweater and had a secretary—was very different from that of the Capuchins. The Salesians dressed well and were perfectly integrated in Manaus middle-class society.

"Sure, I know our brother Cravero," he said.

"Where does he live?"

"I don't have the address, you'll have to ask Padre Mario. You'll find him in a parish church not far from here."

Our search was getting long and complicated, but since we'd gotten that far, we weren't going to give up. Padre Mario eventually told us he knew the address, so we managed to track down Cravero. It was dusk and we invited the two priests for a good dinner of Amazon fish at a restaurant on the Rio Negro. After exchanging civilities, we enjoyed a memorable night of stories and laughter. We told the two about our afternoon adventure, and with great ceremony handed Cravero the food parcel and the letter from his mother. He thanked us and joined us for a drink, over which we told him about the difference we had noted between the Capuchins and the Salesians. We also explained to our two guests how, a few days earlier in the small town of Olinda, we had been to a *terreiro* to take part in a macumba ritual. The *mãe de Santo*[15] involved us in the ceremony and, agnostic though we were, we decided that this ritual religious practice was deserving of respect and curiosity. Padre Mario and Cravero nodded

---

[15] Literally "mother-of-the-saint," a priestess in the syncretic Afro-Brazilian religions of Candomblé, Umbanda, and Quimbanda.

but seemed a little uncomfortable. At the end of the night, as we peppered him with questions about his life in Manaus and why he hadn't been in touch with his relatives, a slightly sheepish Cravero asked, "Will you still be here tomorrow? I'd like you to come to see me. I'll write a reply to my dear mamma tonight." The next day we went to have breakfast with him. He welcomed us with a cup of very good coffee, then told us to go with him into the next room. There, to our astonishment, he unveiled a large macumbeiro's altar with images of the Orixa goddesses, some depicted as Jesus and Saint George, native arrows, the *preto velho*,[16] and all manner of fetishes. Cravero, a Salesian priest, had become a *pai de santo*![17]

He explained that this was the only form of spirituality known and recognized by the locals, that it contained elements of Catholicism, that he couldn't and wouldn't preach them anything else. He had adapted his vocation as a spiritual guide to the circumstances. He was fascinated by these rites and their significance, finding in them the fulfillment of all the reasons he had set out for Brazil in the first place. His wasn't a renunciation, but rather a cultivated way of embracing local customs, of integrating completely and performing his mission. He was one of them, a man of the people, and he was a much more effective preacher than the Capuchin ensconced in his monastery or the Salesian at the service of Manaus high society. We were surprised at first, but we were not shocked, and it was with great pleasure that we continued our tour of Manaus and Amazonia with Cravero as our guide. He helped us discover places from points of view that we would never have imagined. We subsequently kept in touch with him.

---

[16] Literally "old black man," the wise, kindly spirit of a slave who died or was killed in captivity.

[17] Literally "father-of-the-saint," a priest in the syncretic Afro-Brazilian religions of Candomblé, Umbanda, and Quimbanda.

He was no longer recognized by his congregation and the Church, of course, but he continued to live the life he had chosen and loved. We later heard he had gotten married and had children and was a respected guide in his new community.

This is what I mean by the power of diversity, the power of other places, of other lifestyles, of other languages—of alternative ways of interpreting reality. It is fascination, not only intellectual, with forms of music that are poles apart, curiosity for land cultivation techniques at once ancient and modern, for different ways of relating with nature, with the cosmos, with the unfathomable. And, of course, ways of eating and gastronomic cultures, rites, habits, and customs that may transmute into sensational discoveries, if you don't see them or live them day by day.

If you marry diversity as your guide, and if you see it as profound respect for others, it is capable of conquering without reserve—in other words, of converting you to a freer, happier life. Cravero, the missionary convert to Brazilian spiritual syncretism, is a symbol of how diversity can free unthought-of energies, of how it is the driving force that moves the world, both culturally and biologically. Defending diversity, promoting it at every level, using it as a reason for exchange and meeting—these are the most easily available tools for designing a change in paradigm with liberated gastronomy.

So let us free diversity and see what happens. It makes us vital and creative, and it generates respect for other identities— something we need a lot of!—translating into care for the earth. Nature itself tells us that a system with a high level of biodiversity has greater chances of surviving, evolving, and propagating, is healthier and richer, is better able to cope with the adversities that come its way.

Diversity is a promise for the future, the only seriously ecological method of addressing existence. It is the very dimension of life. Unfortunately, there have long been forces at work to mortify it, to reduce it, to level it, to erase it. They use the pretext that diversity is chaotic, as if they felt obliged to reduce the uncertainty that is part of life. Yet, looking closer, uncertainty for the enemies of diversity is merely uncertainty over whether they can make money or not.

# CHAPTER 2

# WE AREN'T FREE ON THE FREE MARKET

In this book I have, to some extent, played with the word "freedom" and all its possible meanings, but now the moment has come to play a "negative-sum game." In the last few decades, neoliberal theory has dusted off the old economic doctrine of the free market, which, much questioned after the 1929 stock market crash, has now returned to the fore. Globalization has increasingly fostered this model so that the economies of the most powerful countries intersect and are mutually dependent, so much so that when one of these enters into crisis—witness what is happening today to the so-called PIGS (Portugal, Italy, Greece, Spain)—outside help has to be called in to avert a domino effect. This mechanism is hard to reconstruct for anyone not *au fait* with economics, but when it is set into motion everyone notices. Here in Italy we have been experiencing it firsthand for at least a couple of years now. The situation is pretty dramatic and we are certainly feeling its consequences.

I am not an economist and I do not want to venture too far into a critique of the free market system, whose detractors include more important, much better qualified people than myself (Amartya Sen[18] is the first name that comes to mind). But I can see what the system has done and is doing to food, and it does not look all that free to me. I do not wish to suggest we change its name—though, since it is a lie, maybe that might not be a bad idea—but I really would like food to leave the free market and no longer be treated like other goods. If food is to join company with freedom, then it must not be subject to an economic doctrine that is wreaking so much harm.

Food is alive and gives life. We have seen how complex the story behind every food is, how many fallouts it has in the most disparate fields, which, coincidentally, encompass all the spheres of human rights and, incidentally, the environment. (If men and women have inalienable rights as living beings, why don't other living systems—ecosystems, rivers, seas, mountains, farm crops—have them, too?) It is palpably a colossal injustice for food to be subject to the rules of the free market as we know it and as it manifests itself. The aim is to make it a standardized commodity, controllable at every stage in its supply chain, as if it were just any other industrial product: seriality as the opposite of diversity, seriality as the possibility of absolute control. According to its theoretical principles, the free market should reward the best and support those who comply with the laws of supply and demand. But especially in the food field, it practices a ruthless selection that leaves no scope either for diversity or, hence, for freedom.

The rules of the free market have accelerated the standardization of food in the world at a lightning rate, making food

---

[18] Amartya Kumar Sen (1933–), Indian economist and philosopher, winner of the Nobel Prize for Economics in 1998.

potentially the same everywhere, progressively erasing biodiversity, traditions, and food cultures, hence jeopardizing the subsistence of many human beings. The free market is a place where we allow almost one billion people to suffer malnutrition and hunger without anyone being scandalized about the fact or doing anything concrete to stop it. It is a place where we sit back and look on as 40 percent of our food is wasted every day. The fact is that this waste is functional to the system, increasing consumption and making the economy "go around." Yet food waste is the sickest thing humankind has ever invented. Hunger and waste are two sides of a logic that wants to force our rural areas to produce more—often using world hunger as a justification—to increase the competitiveness of national agricultures, to make countries place the priority on exports over the well-being of their citizens. All of this spawns absurd situations, such as that of Mexico, for example, which imports 33 percent of the maize it consumes, or of Indonesia which, in some years, imports 40 percent of its rice. These two countries are incredible cradles of biodiversity, but are forced to buy in their principal crops from outside. This is utter madness! The prices of the imported crops, moreover, often are competitive with those of the locally grown ones, and thus undermine the domestic market, ruining the poorest farmers, or at any rate, the farmers who—perhaps driven by the so-called Green Revolution of the 1960s—have been deceived into gambling everything they own on monocultures of commercial hybrids.

The case of Indonesia is exemplary and deserves some explanation. Here I have to thank Helianti Hilman, an Indonesian woman involved in the Slow Food and Terra Madre network, who recently became a member of our International Council. Helianti is seeking to safeguard her country's biodiversity through commercialization. She is a member of the Slow Food Bali convivium and, in partnership with other people, has set up

Javara, a platform that sells endangered traditional Indonesian foods online. The work she does with communities producing traditional rice varieties is very important indeed. It transpires that up to the 1960s, before the government-driven Green Revolution to "modernize" the country's agriculture, there were seven thousand rice varieties in Indonesia. In just a few years since the imposition of commercial hybrids, classic white rices that we are all roughly familiar with, thousands of varieties have been lost—all of them easy to identify insofar as they are red, black, purple, and yellow. Today Helianti and her colleagues have succeeded in saving more than three hundred of these old varieties and market about thirty of them, not of course on the international circuits of the free market, but locally through intense promotion work and across the web. The team is now working to one day sell the other varieties on a larger scale.

It is very important to provide these rice varieties with a commercial outlet, to protect not only the varieties themselves but also the communities that cultivate them. The surprising thing is that these varieties adapt to the most diverse conditions: in the mountains at various altitudes, in dry, almost desert climates, in the shade or in open sunlight, in natural swamps. The native rice is generally not an aquatic plant as we Italians know it. Some varieties do not even require irrigation and communities are skilled at cultivating them. Designed to be cultivated in water to better absorb the chemicals they are sprayed with, they take a little longer to grow than commercial hybrids. Helianti has done a meticulous job, traveling to meet old people who were continuing to grow old varieties in pots to preserve their seeds, threatened with arrest and imprisonment by the government if they refused to switch to the "modern" hybrids. She went to visit communities such as that of the natives of Kasepuhan Ciptagelar in western Java, which has been part of the Terra Madre network for many years. This indigenous people has been cultivating the same rice varieties in their isolated territory for 650 years. They have handed down the seeds over the centuries and have such great respect for Mother Earth—which they venerate in their cosmogony—that they consider its fruits to be sacred. For them it is a taboo to commercialize the seeds, which can be exchanged only in cases of necessity. They cultivate their rice following the signs of the stars, praying, using only the organic manure produced by animals. This may sound like a quaint, inefficient, random approach to the advocates of modernity in agriculture, yet in more than six centuries of history, documented by knowledge handed down by word of mouth, this indigenous people has never experienced a bad year or a famine—or, at least, they cannot remember one. Their rice is so well integrated in the local context that it never risks failing or leaving them without food. They are not hungry and they are free. This aspect of the Kasepuhan Ciptagelar community is very significant because the 40 percent rice imports I spoke of for Indonesia refers to bad years. Since Indonesia is one of the world's largest consumers of rice, much of its national production is earmarked for the domestic market, but the diffusion of commercial hybrids is no guarantee against shortages caused by unforeseen atmospheric events. On the contrary, the standardization of rice varieties means that an unlucky year impacts all national production and that Indonesia, the home of rice, is forced to import its staple food. With their colors, aromas, textures, and versatility in the kitchen, the rice varieties collected and sold by Helianti are instead a feast of diversity, hence a guarantee for the future.

Diversity is not just the exotic charm of ancestral food products cultivated with archaic techniques and, obviously, uncompetitive on the free market. It is the very life of the community, the valorization of indigenous knowledge and economics, of the role of women (always to the fore in these forms of agriculture), of the elders as stewards of skills and history. It is an insurance policy on the future.

It is, interestingly, biological and human diversity that assure the food security of these populations, without ejecting them from their cultural and environmental context—as, alas, was the case of the many people who were forced to obey government diktats in the past—to chase after the purported improvements of the Green Revolution or agroindustry's most recent contrivances, meaning standardization with varieties that subsequently prove fragile if they are not cultivated in a certain way and with the use of dedicated chemicals; the risk of famine as a result of price crashes on international markets or changes in weather conditions that hybrids are unable to tolerate; and supposed higher production yields. Are these improvements? True, commercial hybrids yield more and faster and they may even bring in more cash in good years. But today, Indonesia's staple food, rice, is no longer all that different from the rice produced elsewhere in Southeast Asia, controlled as it is by global markets and by those who sell it and its seeds to cultivate in the best way possible. It is now part of the free market but it is not free. After devastating one of the most important examples of biodiversity, not only for Indonesia but for all humanity, it poses a threat to the community. Which is why I say: let us free food from the free market.

# CHAPTER 3
# THE WASTECONOMY

In September 2011, I made a tour of Germany, visiting Slow Food convivia, Terra Madre communities, and activists involved in various projects. The main "excuse" for the trip was the launch of the Teller Statt Tonne (Plate Not Waste) initiative at two separate events in Stuttgart and Berlin. These were open-air gatherings to which 1,000 and 2,000 people, respectively, came along to eat free meals knocked together with surplus leftover food that would otherwise have ended up in garbage cans. These happenings are still being organized with great success all over the country and Teller Statt Tonne is now one of Slow Food Germany's flagship events. Similar praiseworthy initiatives are underway in other countries: in the United Kingdom, the network that gravitates around the writer Tristram Stuart, author of *Waste: Uncovering the Global Food Scandal*; in Italy, the work of many specialized associations; throughout the English-speaking world, the so-called "freegans network," whose followers practice a strong form of existentialist provocation by eating only still-edible food salvaged from garbage bins. The Slow Food Youth Movement (SFYM) is a world network of young people that has grown up inside Slow Food and Terra Madre. It organizes occasional and hugely enjoyable Disco Salad and Disco Soup events, in which youngsters, entertained by disc jockeys and bands, concoct and eat soups and salads with factory or market leftovers, thus turning their action against waste into a celebration. On the last Italian Slow Food Day, on May 25, 2013, at around half past five in the afternoon, a group of young people in Turin went to the city's Piazza Madama Cristina and Via Nizza street markets to rummage for discarded vegetables. They collected enough of them to fix a salad for about a hundred people in the Parco del Valentino, on the banks of the Po River, in a collective meal that was followed by dancing. Similar Slow Food Youth Movement happenings are frequently organized in Italy, The Netherlands, France, and Germany during our network's major events.

Let me return to my trip to Germany. I, too, helped collect food for the two evening events in Stuttgart and Berlin—and I went out into the fields to do it. I'm not joking: it is in the fields that food waste begins. Food is not only salvaged just before it expires from the garbage bins of supermarkets, or at street markets when they close at the end of the day. No, it is also to be found on farms, including organic farms like the one belonging to the man I went to visit. It is food that no one wants because it does not respond to the characteristics demanded by the organized large-scale distribution system.

So it was that I found myself picking cabbage on Axel Szilleweit's farm in Brandenburg. It was September, when in Germany they obviously do not grow the same things as we do in Italy. There it was the season for cabbage and what we Italians consider "winter" vegetables. As we walked around his fields, I noted in Axel's voice—though he was speaking in German—the same pride that I have always heard among farmers at every latitude when they are showing you their land. Axel plays an active role in the Slow Food movement and has attended Terra Madre meetings in Turin on various occasions. He sells his sizable output of organic produce at farmers' markets within a twenty kilometer or so radius of his farm and to the organized large-scale distribution system.

In Germany, organic produce has an immense market, and demand is so high that domestic production fails to meet it completely. A lot of certified organic produce is thus imported, especially from Italy, one of the largest organic producers in Europe. A recent Bonn University study shows that the sales of organic foods in Germany increased threefold between 2006 and 2012, and that Germans spend about 70 euros a year per capita on organic food, a total of 7 billion euros. Though the area of land cultivated with organic crops doubled in the six years taken into account by the study, only 6.3 percent of the total available land in Germany is untainted by pesticides and chemical fertilizers.

Given this market situation, Axel's business ought to be booming. But in the fields near his farmhouse, he bent over and, in the space of thirty seconds, picked two cabbages. He then showed them to me. One was perfectly compact with jagged-edged leaves; perfectly round and fleshy with thick veins, it looked like a photo out of a catalogue. The second, slightly stunted with spoiled outer leaves, was less impressive; it looked like the first's down-at-heel brother. This is what Axel told me:

> Look, there are good-looking cabbages and ugly cabbages. But do you want to know something? These two are equally good to eat. I can sell the good-looking one, the ugly one . . . no way. Sometimes 50 percent of what I harvest stays here on the farm because it doesn't match up to the aesthetic characteristics listed in the tables large-scale distribution uses to select purchases and fix prices. In these cases, the price is zero and they simply refuse to buy my

cabbages. Which is why I'm pleased about initiatives like Teller Statt Tonne, which avoids wasting food that has cost me the same hard work and passion as all the rest of the stuff I grow.

Last year the London-based Institution of Mechanical Engineers published the results of research into food waste worldwide. The fact that the study was promoted by the association in question is an indication of how the problem is starting to make itself felt in public opinion even in a country like Great Britain, which has sacrificed its traditional food production on the altar of agroindustrial and free market "efficiency," only to discover that 30 percent of its crops remain unharvested—for precisely the same reason that Axel's cabbages remain unsold.

Then there is the problem of individual domestic waste caused by poor home economics or to the special offers of supermarkets—"two for the price of one," for example—which induce us to buy more than we really need at below-cost prices in the hope that we will buy more of the products on display. But that's not all.

A report entitled *Global Food, Waste Not, Want Not* suggests that, depending on geographical area, from 30 percent to 50 percent of food produced in the world—the equivalent of 1.2 to 2 billion tons—never ends up in human stomachs. One might imagine that the problem of waste affects only industrialized countries like Great Britain, but actually the free market and consequent consumerism have also struck elsewhere, sometimes in the most unlikely places. Returning to rice, in Southeast Asia from 38 percent to 80 percent of production—the equivalent of 180 tons a year—is lost along the supply chain, especially during transport. Here inadequate infrastructure causes losses that range from 45 percent in China to 80 percent in Vietnam. Africa, too, has enormous problems—inefficient harvesting, disastrous transport systems, the virtual nonexistence of a temperature-controlled supply chain, and lack of familiarity with the rules of "modern" distribution—meaning that food is wasted even in the places where it is most needed.

It is incredible how a system designed to reduce diversity, increase productivity, and distribute efficiently from centralized structures manages to "lose food" at every turn. Not to mention the fact that not only food but also energy, fertile land, and water are wasted as well. The Water Footprint Network calculates the amount of water used in the productive cycle of food. For example, to produce a kilo of beef "costs" 15,415 liters of water, whereas a kilo of chocolate takes 17,196 liters, a kilo of bread 1,608 liters, a glass of wine 109 liters, and a kilo of rice 2,497 liters. The figures are calculated by counting the use of water along the supply chain, from the cultivation of primary ingredients to processing. This means that in Southeast Asia alone, where 180 million tons of rice are lost every year, the number of liters of water wasted is equivalent to 180 million times 2,497. The figures will make your pocket calculator run amok, and it won't be the only thing to do so!

The system itself is sheer folly, judging food by its price and not by its value, by its appearance and not by its actual characteristics, expecting to increase production by standardizing varieties with intensive cultivation techniques, while half of what is produced is thrown away—all this while a billion people are suffering from hunger and malnutrition. Furthermore, the diversity of nature and the human culture that is closely intertwined with it is being limited in an attempt to channel everything into the furrows of a certainty that will always be vain—an illusory control that only multiplies problems and creates new ones. The "wasteconomy" is the free market, the opposite of diversity and the opposite of life.

I know I will draw criticism from those who regard me as refractory to progress, but I am no longer prepared to tolerate these abominations. I do not want indigenous communities to adapt to us and our iniquitous methods, I do not want the role of women—fundamental in every nonindustrialized agricultural economy—to be debased, for youngsters to have no prospects, not even of returning to the land, for the elderly to be forgotten or marginalized. These people have strength, knowledge, passion, tradition on their side, they are different from how the system would like them to be, they represent the value we want to liberate—diversity. These are the people who can create a new system that will allow humanity to nourish itself, which is why it is vital to protect them, the biodiversity they use, and the forms of sustainable agriculture they practice. It is also why we want to see new distribution systems that no longer contemplate waste. This does not mean returning to the past, it means designing the future. Do not tell me that, in this way, there will not be enough food for all, for a world population that is growing vertiginously. Maybe it will not be a sufficient source of profit for those who would like to control our sustenance globally and locally, for those who do not want food to be free. But the fact is that there will never be enough food as long as waste is the true economic driving force of the world food sector.

# CHAPTER 4

# UNPAIRING THE CARDS

A nyone familiar with the Italian card games *scopa* or *scopone scientifico* will know the meaning of the term "*sparigliare le carte*," literally "unpairing the cards." *Scopone* is played by four players, two against two. The members of the non-dealing team have to take as many tricks as they can with cards of different values—four and three take seven for example, six and two take eight—the aim being to leave an odd number of cards on the table. If they fail to do so, it is likely that all the cards will go to the dealing team, since it always plays the last card. "Unpairing the cards" opens up new possibilities, allowing the non-dealers to win the hand and the dealers to right the situation. In other words, it is a destabilizing tactic that makes the game more interesting and the players more creative.

"Unpairing the cards," turning things upside down, is a metaphor that is often used in the Slow Food offices when we are developing new projects or seeking to revitalize others that are floundering. It is also a rule we follow in our day-to-day activity because, historically speaking, it has always stimulated us to put something extra into our work, to stoke our imagination. The picture I have painted of a homogenizing, wasteful global system is like a dud hand for the non-dealers in a *scopa* game. "Unpairing the cards" is a good way of averting any risk to biodiversity, food communities, small farmers, fishers, artisans, marginal areas, young people, old people, and indigenous people—to "good, clean, and fair" food as a right (and duty) for all. But how does one go about unpairing the cards in a structured system driven by multinational powers and governments that are always rather passive in this regard?

The key is to work on a local scale because it is here that it is possible to protect and render fertile both the biodiversity of nature and the cultural diversity that results from it. For food culture—and not only food culture—has to be formed in connection with context, with the resources available in a local area, with ecosystems, with one's relations with one's neighbors. In this way it can be stratified and solidified and transformed into what we call tradition and which ultimately constitutes identity. Diversity is a fundamental ingredient of identity, even though some people would have us believe that identity is a set of characteristics, fixed and immobile, rooted in a sort of unique and extreme point of purity. But its real roots branch out underground and move away from the plant to explore. The same applies if we link identity to the past. As I shall never tire of repeating, it is always the fruit of exchange, a good cure for intolerance and a guiding idea that opens up very interesting scenarios for our future. In an age of globalization, this exchange has potentialities unprecedented in human history; suffice it to think of the way we travel and communicate today. This is why it is mistaken to say that we are against globalization, as Lawrence Osborne did in the *New York Times* article in which he described us as "eco-gastronomes."

The fact is that globalization can become an opportunity, a veritable driving force, provided, that is, we fill it with very rich fuel—by which of course I mean diversity. Only if homogenization reigns, can globalization become a negative force. So the work that has to be done is neither for or against globalization, which is a process that cannot be arrested and that, like latter-day Luddites, only stick-in-the-mud traditionalists, nostalgic for the old as an end in itself, would ever gainsay. If we want to unpair the cards, what we have to do is fill the engine with the right fuel and make it run well, thus setting free the diversity in the globalized world.

Mark my words, when I talk of diversity I am not only referring to the traditions and biodiversity that deserve to be saved, but also to anything new, anything good, clean, and fair that comes into being when cultural exchange becomes a way of rethinking one's local area and creating something that was not there before. After all, only the naive or incompetent believe that tradition, just like identity, is fixed and immobile, like an exhibit locked in a showcase in a museum. Everything is in motion; what is important is that it goes in the right direction.

Early one morning in 2003, I called a few of my closest collaborators to my office to tell them about a new idea I had had. It was the idea that one day would materialize as Terra Madre, and I had been up all night trying to find the best way of unpairing the cards in the game we were playing at that time. In those days we used to organize the Slow Food Award for Biodiversity, which had brought us into contact with communities that were doing an incredible job, but we could not involve all of them in the event. We used to receive hundreds of nominations every year for the award, but for purely economic reasons, the award organizers were able to invite only a few jury members from the winning communities. In my opinion, that wasn't enough, so I unpaired the cards. Let's invite all these communities, I said, let's look for even more, let's build up their economies so that they can afford to come—we are talking about farmers who had never left their villages in their lives—let's organize the greatest ever world meeting of sustainable food producers. The number I put forward was 10,000, and eventually 6,000 people turned up at the first meeting, which we staged in Turin in 2004. The event has been repeated every two years since then, but, in reality, right from the word "go" it constituted a network of 2,000 food communities in almost every corner of the world—a million people, maybe more—all with the same idea of food, firmly based in their local areas and on their day-to-day labor: growing crops, raising livestock, fishing, processing, selling what they produce through channels outside the free-market system. It was a simple but unique idea. Inside the network there are some people who study food with a holistic approach, and there are others who keep it alive with music, orality, and every form of gastronomic skill.

In terms of the number of people involved, Terra Madre immediately grew bigger than Slow Food itself. Indeed, one might say that it is Terra Madre that contains Slow Food in its institutional and associational form. What counts, though, is not the form but the substance, by which I mean the exaltation, celebration, and capitalization, through exchange, of the vastest range of food-related cultures and skills in the world. Terra Madre is arguably the only, real and non-virtual, glocal subject that exists, adapting global products to local contexts, connecting, ideally and physically, all the earth's gastronomic diversities. If we put together all the knowledge and production of the people in this network of ours, there is no food multinational to match it, nothing comparable in terms of volumes produced, of wealth, diffusion, and variety. "Unpairing the cards" with our projects, we have found a way of unpairing them at a much higher level that is, fortunately, not excessively self-referential. All we have done is to espouse diversity and trust it, without being really sure of what was going to happen.

I will return to Terra Madre and the network as a key tool of liberation later, but let me add here that we also have other more dedicated and specific tools at our disposal. Such as the Ark of Taste, one of Slow Food's oldest projects, which dates back to 1996. It was the Ark of Taste in fact that, historically speaking, began to give concrete form to our idea of safeguarding biodiversity, subsequently developing into the Slow Food Presidia and Terra Madre. At our association's last international congress we unpaired the cards once again, relaunching the Ark of Taste with a very ambitious target. For the Ark is another phenomenal vehicle for injecting diversity into the veins of the world and the humanity that populates it.

# CHAPTER 5

# AN ARK WITH A CARGO OF 10,000 FOODS

conference organized by Slow Food on December 2, 1996, during the first experimental and limited Salone del Gusto in Turin, was entitled "An Ark of Taste to Save the Universe of Flavors." That was the first time the Noah's Ark metaphor was used to evoke the idea of rounding up traditional endangered or forgotten foods like the pairs of animals in the Bible. In this case, the flood was not universal but "global," a flood that did not inundate and destroy with water but with homogenization, the enemy of diversity.

The idea sketched out at the Turin conference immediately made steps forward. The first was on June 29, 1997, less than a year later, when we published the "Manifesto of the Ark of Taste." I reproduce the whole document below, whose language shows how far Slow Food thinking had developed at that point in time. Its content also reveals plans that were largely implemented in 1998 with the setting up of the Presidia project, which was an even more concrete and efficient way of safeguarding biodiversity. This interesting document reads as follows:

> To protect the small purveyors of fine food from the deluge of industrial standardization; to ensure the survival of endangered animal breeds, cheeses, cold cuts, edible herbs—both wild and cultivated—cereals and fruit; to promulgate taste education; to make a stand against obsessive worrying about hygienic matters, which kills the specific character of many kinds of production; to protect the right to pleasure.

> As spokesmen for culture, the food and wine industry, scientific research, journalism, politics and the institutions, we hope to persuade like-minded people to join us in the pursuit of these objectives. By way of a response to the alarm raised by Slow Food, we are launching:

> An Ark of Taste to Save the Universe of Flavors.

> The Ark of Taste is [ . . . ] a project aimed at safeguarding and promoting small-scale fine food purveyors who are threatened by extinction. The project embraces both the scientific and the promotional sides of the issue.

> From the scientific viewpoint we undertake to:

> · define methods and criteria for research—in particular, outlining the very notion of gastronomic asset, typicality, tradition, and endangered products

> · provide an ethno-botanical and historical characterization of cultivars, local breeds, and products as a measure for the recognition of what is typical and/or traditional

> · promote scientific training of experts in the field at a national level

> · set up a networked data bank managed by a central body for collecting the data progressively obtained on cultivars, breeds, products, research, recipes, producers, restaurants, and so on.

From a promotional viewpoint we undertake to:

- draw up and circulate a list of endangered products—known by the public at large and steeped in symbolic value—so that the struggle to defend them becomes as encompassing as possible

- analyze these products from an organoleptic[19] viewpoint, providing the names and addresses of the remaining producers, and advertise them through the mass-media and specialist publications so that the concept of protection goes hand in hand with that of economic return

- invite consumers to purchase and eat these products, convinced as we are that extinction can be avoided only if they are fully reintroduced into the commercial/food circuit

- identify within each region a series of inns or taverns—to be awarded special recognition—that will become active regional promoters of the Ark products, using them on a daily basis in the preparation of their dishes

- invite major restaurants to select a specific Ark product as their "pet product," protecting and introducing it in certain dishes

- launch a campaign throughout Italy so that each municipality "adopts" an endangered product, thus promoting its production and consumption

- implement in the near future a pilot project on a regional or sub-regional scale with a view to verifying and adjusting methods, schedules, and procedures for the realization of the overall project

- promote projects aimed at teaching taste to young people right from school age, with a view to developing people's organoleptic capacities so that they can recognize quality products and draw the utmost pleasure from them

---

[19] Organoleptic, involving the use of the sense organs.

- prod national institutions into considering the safeguarding of these products—gastronomic assets in general, and
  not just those in danger—as a major goal for the economy
  and integral part of Italy's cultural identity
- associate with similar projects throughout Europe, convinced as we are that protecting typical and/or traditional
  quality food and agricultural products must become a
  transnational operation, given the fact that markets and
  strategies are growing increasingly globalized and standardized.

Approved on *June 29, 1997*

In 1999, the Ark Scientific Commission was set up to identify
categories and selection criteria—organoleptic excellence, native
varieties or breeds, limited numbers, production by small-scale
agriculture, at risk of extinction—for the foods to be loaded onto
the imaginary vessel that had just been launched. In 2002, to all
intents and purposes, the Ark went international, helping the
Slow Food association to spread the above-mentioned concepts
around the word, and, above all, to single out food products at
exceptional risk, even in the most isolated places, to add to the
Presidia project, its "armed wing," which saves foods from the
flood and offers new prospects to entire local areas. Today there
are national Ark Commissions throughout the Slow Food galaxy,
as well as an International Commission that directs and oversees
research work. The selection criteria have since been updated
and, though they have not changed a great deal, I believe they
have improved:

1. Nominations for inclusion on the Ark must be food products and may include: domestic species (plant varieties,
   ecotypes, indigenous animal breeds and populations),
   wild species (only if tied to methods of harvesting, processing, and traditional uses), and processed products.

2. Products must be of distinctive quality in terms of taste. Taste quality is defined in the context of local traditions and uses.

3. Products must be linked to a specific area, to the memory and identity of a group, and to local traditions.

4. Products must be produced in limited quantities.

5. Products must be at risk of extinction.

The key words have changed since the 1990s and the document no longer uses the word "excellence" to define quality. The most significant and important part for me is the footnote:

> It is essential to interpret and apply the criteria with regard to the specific local situation of the product, always respecting the cultural, social, geographical, economic, and political differences of the communities who preserve the products.

Music to my ears! The note is saying that diversity—not only the biological diversity of breeds and varieties, but also the diversity of the context in which these live and have evolved: what we might call human diversity—is being sought after and respected. Unfortunately, the Ark of Taste failed to accomplish its original intentions and turned into a mere catalogue, albeit an important one. Through the Foundation for Biodiversity that was set up in the meantime to manage and source the funds needed for projects on the subject, the focus of protection as such shifted to the inchoate Presidia. In October 2012, during the Slow Food International Congress in Turin, the association's management bodies were replaced, and many of the Terra Madre food community delegates were brought in, thereby expanding international representation considerably. It was on that occasion that I had an idea, or rather three ideas. Here they are one by one.

Won over by the variety of people, nationalities, cultures, ages, trades, and ethnic groups who flocked to Turin for the Salone del

Gusto and Terra Madre, which were being held simultaneously on the same days as the congress, I wanted to find a way for all this diversity to embody the true substance of the movement. I wanted it to be liberated in all its wonder and all its might. I listened, rapt, to the speeches that were carrying the voices of the communities of every continent, from ultra-anthropized urban realities to the most remote rural areas. It was there that I was able to shake hands for the first time with Helianti Hilman and many other people I had previously only heard about who, under the banner of the Slow Food snail, are carrying on their revolutionary work in silence. Anyway, after my usual sleepless night and to the surprise of many of those present, I suggested we revive the Ark of Taste, a project that had been put aside to develop others, as one of our key projects for the future, again with a very precise aim: to load 10,000 foods onto the Ark by 2016 (the number stands at 2,500).

Another two objectives set on that occasion—and here we come back to my three ideas—also had the number 10,000 as their final target, and I shall return to them later. When they think back to the 2012 International Congress and the three motions, which were voted unanimously, and with a certain enthusiasm, by all the delegates present, Slow Food insiders speak confidentially about the "three ten thousands." We had unpaired the cards again, setting ourselves difficult, faraway objectives. If we are to achieve the change we want so much, we will certainly have to work hard—to go the proverbial extra mile. But there is no turning back; what an IT expert would label Slow Food 2.0 has now been born.

Diversity remains the cornerstone, the source of life and future. Twenty years after it was first launched, the Ark of Taste is ready to set sail again, to draw up new selection criteria to broaden our horizons and release hitherto unimagined, salvific energies.

# CHAPTER 6

# NEW DIVERSITY, NEW BIODIVERSITY

Through my work, I have had the good fortune to travel often to the United States over the last 25 years, on average once a year, maybe more. They have always been very much journeys of gastronomic discovery, naturally enough, and my guides have always been Slow Food members, the number of whom is increasing all the time. Some of these people are still involved in the movement, others have left but are moving in parallel directions. I had the opportunity in the past to discover nascent phenomena that have since become veritable North American and international trends; to reflect upon the relationship between exchange and identity; to understand that the larger any negative trend is, the more it will be countered by an opposite trend capable of subverting the apparent order of things. It is amazing how rapidly American society is changing. Every time I go to the States I see how the home of fast food and industrial agriculture, the place that has "regaled" us with so many of the elements that have combined to make the world food system the grave problem it is today (GMOs, commercial hybrids, DDT, pesticides as a by-product of arms production), is also where the concept of tradition and biodiversity evolve fastest in very creative forms that offer an entirely different perspective from the Eurocentrism that lives on inside every native of the Old Continent.

I shall return more than once to my experiences in the USA because "always respecting the cultural, social, geographical, economic and political differences of the communities who preserve [ . . . ] products," means that one cannot look only to the past and its sediments for the necessary (bio) diversity. We also have to be clever interpreters of a present that is redefining itself all the time.

During my first trips to the United States, my enlightened guides taught me about remote traditions whose roots stretch all around the world. But, at the same time, they made me aware of how industrial food production had been taken to extremes unknown at that time—it was the late 1980s—in Europe, extremes that were eliminating or turning many of America's albeit young gastronomic habits into museum pieces. Everywhere I heard the same refrain, "There used to be this, we used to make that." It was hard to find beer other than the leading two or three industrial brands, impossible to eat cheese that didn't taste of the plastic it was wrapped in, while especially in the big cities the vegetables, serially produced like nuts or bolts, were generally flavorless. The first Slow Food members were very committed to saving the little that was left in their communities and towns and cities. They would proudly take me to establishments with at least a century of history behind them that still preserved—sometimes in a very sterile manner, without a great deal of quality—the recipes "of the house." No that everything was awful, of course, but good places to eat were exceptions in a panorama that held out little hope for the future. The accounts of my journeys that I used to take back to the association in Italy inevitably brought out these serious problems and the homogenization behind them.

Then suddenly, from the 1990s onward, everything seemed to change. The work of my friend Alice Waters, who, in 1971, opened her Chez Panisse restaurant in Berkeley, California, set an organic revolution into motion, changing the food habits of many Americans, and was starting to bear unforeseen fruits. Her pupils were colonizing the kitchens of every city in every state in the union with their sustainable practices. Organic farmers seemed to be everywhere, most of them young people who had returned to the land and came across to their contemporaries as being cool. Farmers' markets and the culture of local food were beginning to spread and have since established themselves as the norm from coast to coast. Like outlaws in the Wild West, some individuals were daring enough to make cheese with raw milk, a practice banned by a law clearly sponsored by industrial lobbies. With true pioneer spirit, they were subverting the system—and were doing so under threat of heavy sanctions. But that was not all.

In 1998, I made a very interesting trip to New York City, where I was taken on a tour of its gastronomic wonders by Patrick Martins, director of Slow Food USA at the time, and Garrett Oliver, the Slow Food New York convivium leader. I met many other members, some of whom were quite important people, and all of them made it their business to let me live the atmosphere of the Big Apple the way true New Yorkers have been doing for generations. I was welcomed as a guest in luxury apartments and converted lofts, I dined in high-class restaurants and in marvelous little ethnic eateries off the normal tourist routes, I ate so-called fast food—excellent hamburgers and sensational street foods—with gusto, and drank in bars where the art of cocktail-making reached heights that left me speechless. I visited the city's first farmers' markets, like the historic one in Union Square, and I realized immediately that a profound transformation was underway.

What had once been a small vanguard of people who had decided to put food at the center of their lives was morphing into a broader, more united nationwide movement. What surprised me most about that journey was the discovery of a nascent new diversity of microbreweries and local beers; I found that exemplary.

Garrett Oliver had worked as brewmaster at the Brooklyn Brewery—a brand you see in virtually all the bars and restaurants in New York—since its foundation, eleven years earlier. Then the brewery was not exceptionally powerful: it was medium-sized and still had many of the features of a craft business. Today it is huge and its products are distributed widely—though it is still a small-fry compared to the two or three industrial brands I mentioned above.

Garrett took me around the brewery's first historic plant in Williamsburg, Brooklyn, and introduced me to the world of American craft brewing. In subsequent trips to America, I have seen how every American urban center—from the great metropolises to small towns—has a beer of its own, often with a name that conjures up the area where it is produced. In a few years from the time when only a handful of poor-quality labels were available, a phenomenon had exploded that had given life to what we might term a new productive biodiversity, whose roots reached back to traditional beer-making countries, such as Belgium, Germany, and Great Britain, and which is now building new identities around an exchange of know-how and skill. It was no coincidence that Garrett, an exceptional brewmaster, had studied in Europe for a number of years.

A craft microbrewery phenomenon has since sprung up in Italy, which in recent years has, proportionally speaking, outstripped that in the USA for diffusion and growth. It began in

1996 with Le Baladin, a brewery set up by Teo Musso in the village of Piozzo—again in the Langa area of Piedmont—and today we have 500 craft breweries nationwide against 1,700 or more in the USA. Even if it cannot be defined as traditional and is only now becoming "typical," this is the new diversity I like. This swelling—hence not dwindling—new wave has to be protected, followed, and respected, exactly as if it were a product at risk. Moreover, many of the people involved, from Garrett in New York to Teo in Piozzo, have shown themselves to be the firmest supporters of the battle for the protection of biodiversity, precisely because they are aware that, far from representing competition for their businesses, it offers an opportunity. Proof of the fact is the network of brewers that has built up worldwide, all friends united together in alliances against the standardization and homogenization that the major beer multinationals aggressively impose as a matter of course on every continent. Even India, in the three years since craft brewing licenses became freely available in 2010 (previously craft brewing had been banned), we have witnessed the miracle of the multiplication of first-rate beer across the nation.

If it is to release all its energy, this new food diversity has to be nurtured and liberated. It is the same diversity that developed in Piedmont among the small Langa wine producers—innovators and traditionalists alike—who reacted to the methanol scandal by resuscitating their sector and putting it on the world map. It is the same diversity that was created in the USA by outlaw raw milk cheesemakers and, as we shall see, in other countries, proving that it is possible to produce excellent local cheeses, maybe inspired by European techniques (not the phonies that are usually the preserve of big industry), which, albeit young, have a dignity of their own and, though they have little history behind them, are nonetheless excellent for anyone who knows anything about gastronomy. The Ark of Taste concept is thus capable of evolving into something more complex still.

# CHAPTER 7

# SAY CHEESE!

have to say that I am always happy when, every two years in September, Slow Food organizes "Cheese. Milk in All Its Shapes and Forms" in Bra. The event, the largest in the world dedicated to cheese and all things dairy, came into being in 1997 as a result of a wager with the Bra town council. Today—let me add with a touch of good old Piedmontese regional pride—it is the feather in the town's cap. It is made all the more enjoyable by the fact that it is held not in the pavilions of an exhibition center, but "colonizes" and occupies all the main streets and squares in the town, which reveals an amazing capacity to welcome hordes of visitors from many different countries. There is a party-like atmosphere, a mixture between that of my favorite secular places of worship, namely our country fairs in Piedmont—like the legendary Fat Ox Fair, which has been held in the nearby village of Carrù for centuries, and which I never miss—and the *ferias* of Spain, which bring towns and villages to a standstill for whole weeks, transforming them into places of endless celebrations, as spectacular as Holy Week processions, sometimes dangerous and controversial, like the *feria de San Fermin* in Pamplona.

But Cheese is more than just a pleasant way of having a good time in a pretty little Italian provincial town. It has become a place for developing and carrying forward Slow Food's work on biodiversity, education, preservation, and promotion; a place where the world of fine cheese, which champions an incredible human and productive diversity, meets every two years to think and plan ahead. It is an occasion in which future trends are elaborated and real changes are forged, some of them epoch-making, such as the campaign for the defense of raw milk cheese, which has achieved and continues to achieve great results. The campaign was first launched at the earliest Cheese events and has been going on for about fifteen years. It was particularly successful in 2001, when we collected over 20,000 signatures in support of the Slow Food Manifesto for the defense of raw milk cheese. The document was drawn up to protect the rights of cheesemakers in countries in which excessively rigid hygiene laws ban or jeopardize their raw milk cheese production. This is a matter of some importance because the pasteurization of milk is, after all, a serious form of homogenization, not only of taste but also of the nutritional and organoleptic properties of milks (I use the plural advisedly) that are processed into cheese, almost always by small or even tiny dairies using artisan methods. All Slow Food Presidia cheeses are made with raw milk. Thanks to the publication of the Manifesto and six triumphal Cheese events in Bra, we have achieved significant success in the United States (defending our outlaw friends and receiving their help), in Ireland, in Great Britain, in Australia, and, more recently, in Brazil and South Africa, where very strict regulations restrict the use of raw milk. Our campaign is continuing and we have no intention of terminating it. We have decided to call it the Cheese Resistance campaign precisely because, in many situations, it is necessary to resist to defend biodiversity.

In many cases, work is being done to defend old cheeses, cheesemaking techniques (shepherds and mountain dairymen are more interesting characters who need to be defended), to raise native animal breeds, to preserve portions of pastureland or areas with a long history of cheesemaking. Now, thanks to the new impulse given by our new target of 10,000 products for loading on the Ark, we are making discoveries in places where even dairy experts would least expect to find them. As in the case of U.S. beer and raw milk cheese, a new diversity is being born and traditions are emerging that few people knew about. Returning to the exemplary cases of Brazil and South Africa, which I cited previously, in the third issue of *Slow* magazine, Maurizio Busca, a collaborator of the Slow Food Foundation for Biodiversity, wrote as follows:

> How many people have tasted South African raw milk cheese or at least heard of it? In Italy probably very few. What might come as a surprise is that, even in South Africa, there aren't many people who would answer in the affirmative. For interest in cheese in general, and raw milk cheese in particular, is a relatively recent phenomenon there. Cheese production in the region has been documented for centuries, but there is no evidence of a real local dairy tradition. Today the cheeses South African dairies sell are mostly their more or less faithful takes on European cheeses, with a few original creations that are the fruit of the experimentation of individual producers.

> Given this premise and that the aim of the Presidia ought to be to protect *traditional* products, the fact that Slow Food is working on a South African Raw Milk Cheese Presidium is bound to raise eyebrows. To understand the significance of the initiative, we have to consider it in relation to its context, observing the country's dairy production with greater attention.

Until a few decades ago, cheese, mainly in the form of Gouda and Cheddar, accounted for a tiny slice of the South African agrifood market. Especially since the 1990s, however, in parallel with the growth of domestic demand, we have witnessed the birth of small and large companies that have not only increased the volume of national production, but have also diversified the supply and improved the quality of products. Average consumption per capita has doubled in the last fifteen years, in shops it is possible to find a growing number of types of cheese, and, more recently, numerous cheese events and competitions have been organized. The South African market is, however, dominated by large milk and cheese companies and national and international distribution chains. There are only a few artisan cheesemakers, and those using raw milk are very rare indeed. There is nothing surprising about this; cheese is a "new" food for the country and a cheese "culture" has only begun to spread recently. Furthermore, the benefits of raw milk and the merits of cheese made with nonpasteurized milk are relatively unknown, and the market for it is so small that the national legislation regulating its production is still somewhat vague.

Which is precisely why Slow Food intends to join the best artisan producers together in a Presidium: to bring the finest national cheeses to the attention of consumers in South Africa and beyond, by supporting the cheesemakers who are laying the bases for what could be a South African tradition of the future.

Tradition of the future, new biodiversity, partly domestic diversity. Two excellent South African cheeses such as Karoo Crumble and Ganzvlei Valstrap, made respectively by Francy Schoeman of the Langbaken farm in Williston and Christopher Metelerkamp of the Ganzvlei farm in Knysna, are based on the same premises. They are both inspired by English Cheddar and are both made from the milk of Jersey cows. Yet they are different because they are made in different places: Karoo Crumble comes from the desert region of Karoo and has notes of hay, hazelnut, and aromatic herbs, and great complexity; Ganzvlei Valstrap comes from a region with heavy rainfall, not far from the ocean, and smacks of the herbs and the scrub on which the cattle graze. Some producers are very concerned with the sustainability of their productive processes: Nipper and Sylvia Thompson, for example, who have been making organic cow's and goat's cheeses by hand since 1986 at their small Wegraakbosch farm at Haenertsburg, where the only electricity they consume is generated by solar panels.

Interesting new discoveries have been made for the Ark in Brazil, too. Here cheese production goes back further in time, having been introduced, obviously, by the Portuguese. Though a real tradition does exist, it is unknown to most people outside production areas, Brazilians included. The most active cheese-making regions are in the south of the country (Serrano and Coloniali) and in the southeast (Minas artesenal) and in the northeast (Calho and by-products such as bottled butter). All these cheeses are made with raw cow's milk, but are very different from one another. The fact that they are made of raw milk constitutes a threat to their very existence. In the state of Minas Gerais, for example, to the north of Rio de Janeiro and São Paulo, 30,000 dairies in the regions of Serro, Alto Parnaíba, Serra de Canastra, and Araxá produce as many as 70,000 tons of cheese every year.

In another article published in *Slow* magazine, Mariana Guimarães writes that:

> Luciano Carvalho Machado, 48, produces Serra da Canastra cheese. There's no point in asking him when he decided to take up the profession: "I grew up with my grandparents, who used to make cheese every day, and before I knew it I was making it myself." His daughter, who is 16, helps him turn out about 15 kilos every day. It is impossible to increase quantity and preserve quality and craftsmanship at the same time. In 2008 the craft cheese

of Minas Gerais was recognized as an "Immaterial Heritage of Brazil" by the Instituto do Patrimônio Historíco e Artístico Nacional (IPHAN) [ . . . ] In spite of the recognition, mineiro craft cheese risked disappearing, since commercializing this heritage outside the Minas Gerais boundaries was against the law. So does that mean that what's good for Minas Gerais isn't good for the rest of the country? Are only mineiros entitled to know and enjoy this national heritage?

This situation has spawned an illegal market, with merchants loading up their cars with raw milk cheese by night and driving down uncovered roads to avoid police checks and reach the markets of São Paulo and Rio de Janeiro, the country's main commercial centers, early the next day.

Another gang of outlaws like my friends in the USA! These are the "discoveries" Slow Food has made with its Ark of Taste, the first fruits—almost immediate—of the new search for 10,000 foods. It is incredible how products such as craft beer and raw milk cheese can become the vehicle of a renaissance based precisely on variety, on the syncretism between cultures and traditions, on the cutting-edge inventiveness and labor of many farmers and artisans who refuse to succumb to the rules imposed by the global food system. It is gratifying to witness all this diversity, not to bask in the glory of reaching the targets set but, above all, because after so many years of commitment one continues to discover that the world is still a cornucopia of emblematic food products, fundamental for the work of us free gastronomes. We are still uplifted by the existence of these foods and the people who unceasingly produce them, making them live, turning them into tradition, adopting them as identity. Just like the food they make, these people deserve to be protected and supported on account of the immense contribution they make to the cause of good, clean, and fair food for everyone on the planet. We have to believe in them and, above all, we have to get to know them.

# CHAPTER 8
# THE LAST?

It has always been believed that small farmers are the "fifth wheel on the wagon" and count for nothing in the social order. It was believed in the past and it is still believed today, all over the world, albeit with varying nuances. Though they oversee our principal source of sustenance, they generally enjoy low prestige, and people have few scruples about jeopardizing their life's work and their survival. But among small farmers, there are some who might be likened to the "spare wheel" of the metaphorical wagon: underestimated, but vital in the event of a breakdown.

In these well-defined categories, there are people who are the last, but they deserve to be the first. In silence, against general indifference, they play a vital role for humanity. Not only should we recognize this, but we ought make it the linchpin of our planning for the future, for our possible futures. I am referring here to women, the elderly, youngsters, and indigenous people.

You only have to travel through any portion of rural Africa to understand what women represent for the economy there. Bent over in the fields, they seem to never stop working. Their oldest children look after the smallest by the sides of the fields, and no men are to be seen. I imagine they are away somewhere doing jobs that require less effort. Women played a central role in Lara in Kenya, the place of the Pumpkin Presidium, as they do in Indonesia, where they are working on the conservation of old rice varieties, coordinated by Helianti Hilman. They account for 43 percent of the agricultural workforce in the so-called developing countries. In the 2011 edition of its *State of Food and Agriculture* report, the Food and Agriculture Organization (FAO) wrote that:

> According to [our] latest estimates, 925 million people are currently undernourished. Closing the gender gap in agricultural yields could bring that number down by as much as 100–150 million people [ . . . ] direct improvements in agricultural output and food security are just one part of the significant gains that could be achieved by ensuring that women have equal access to resources and opportunities [ . . . ] Closing the gender gap in agriculture would put more resources in the hands of women and strengthen their voice within the household—a proven strategy for enhancing the food security, nutrition, education, and health of children. And better fed, healthier children learn better and become more productive citizens. The benefits would span generations and pay large dividends in the future.

Women are the linchpins of the Terra Madre food communities and the Presidium producers. This is why, during Slow Food activities, in particular at the conferences organized during our major events, we seize every possible opportunity to place the onus, substantially and systematically, on the role of women in preserving agricultural biodiversity (they are the main conservers and multipliers of seeds), in creating and guarding traditional culinary skills, and on the ingenuity, passion, and love with which they oversee the domestic economy in the poorest rural societies. If the earth is a mother and not a father, there must be a reason why.

The elderly are, in turn, the stewards of memory, especially in societies that hand down their skills and wisdom orally. They are the only people whose outlook is sufficiently deep, turned simultaneously to past and future. When I went to interview the late Tonino Guerra in December 2010, just over a year before his death at the ripe old age of ninety-two, I wanted to speak to him about the "Granaries of Memory," a multimedia research project of the University of Gastronomic Sciences in Pollenzo that collects interviews with our elders. In its burgeoning archive of learning and wisdom, life stories told firsthand create a bottomless treasure trove of cues for tomorrow. The granary metaphor is not all that different from the Ark one. We are storing the seeds of knowledge, as you would do with grain, to be ready to face times of cultural famine in the future.

My fear is that that famine is already upon us, in which case our granaries are another important factor for the enrichment of diversity. In his house in Pennabilli, Tonino Guerra gently coaxed me into his world of poetry, of attention to small things, of details that convey all the beauty of life. "'Granary' is a new word, a poetic word that confuses one," said the maestro when I pressed him on his ideas about the "Granaries of Memory" project. "I enjoy it when you say something to somebody and, at first, they haven't a clue what you're talking about and you have them confused. Great things are never clear straightaway, they become clear later." Great things are never clear straightaway— that is exactly what I thought after the very first preparatory meeting for Terra Madre, and I now realize it is what occurs to me when I think back, with the benefit of hindsight, to "touring the country" and Milano Golosa. "How do you see a people with no memory?" I asked Guerra. "No such people can exist. Memory is indispensable, and let me tell you something else. When they ask me what history is, what memory is, I always tell the story of my grandfather who, when he was out walking always kept looking backward. I once asked him, '*Nonno*, why do you keep looking back?' and he answered, 'I have to, because that's where the way forward comes from.' So it's right for a people or a person or a country to keep in mind what those who preceded them have given." Tonino was a great character, an immense character, and I miss him a lot. Luckily that conversation was filmed and lives on in the "Granaries of Memory."

Then come young people. I cannot even remember when I started talking about a "return to the land" for the new generations. Here in Europe, the old continent, we have witnessed the depopulation of our countryside: in the postwar years, the rural workforce accounted for about half the total number of workers, but then plummeted to a small percentage. Figures vary country by country, of course; in Italy, for example, there were 3,133,188 agricultural workers in 1982 and only 1,620,844 in 2010. Another worrying trend was the increase in their age, which showed no signs of waning in the first decade of the new century. According to data for the years 2000–2007 released by ISTAT (Italian National Institute of Statistics), the number of farmers under forty years of age dropped from 263,000 to 129,000 and accounted for only 6.2 percent of the total number of agricultural workers. The last few years, however, have recorded a surprising inversion in tendency, with small increases every year; despite the crisis, 2012, for example, recorded an increase of 9 percent. It almost seems as if the general crisis and the drop in employment are among the principal incentives to return to the land, which, slowly but surely, is being seen as a concrete alternative and a prospect for the future.

Maybe it is not only the crisis that is fostering the return. In 2009, I was doing a conference tour of America's prestigious Ivy League universities. In the space of a few days, I visited Harvard, Yale, and Princeton. On each occasion I was faced by a student audience and I always began by asking two questions: "How many of you expect to go and work in the country when you graduate?" and "How many of you are seriously considering becoming farmers?" Well, at the universities that turn out the crème de la crème of scientists, lawyers, and literati, a staggering average 10 percent of youngsters raised their hands: maybe about 40 out of 400, 25 out of 250. I subsequently asked the same questions in Italy but, even in an agrarian institute, only 4 out of 300 students said they wanted to be farmers. We were obviously lagging behind the USA somewhat at that time, but in the last four years something has evidently snapped here, too, considering how agrarian colleges and university agriculture departments are enjoying a boom in enrollments. Not that I am surprised. It is clear to me, in fact, that the wave that is now making the land look like a good prospect for the future has swept in from the United States, where I had already seen that farming was exerting an increasing appeal. It is right for farming and fishing, cheesemaking and artisan food making, to be seen once more as being decent jobs. It is also right that they should offer better prospects than in the time our parents and grandparents, who lived in conditions that would be unacceptable for young people in the twenty-first century and were the root cause of the exodus from the countryside we have witnessed in recent decades. The young people of today have studied, are familiar with new technologies, and spurn the idea of being shackled in precarious office jobs in city offices and fettered in the mechanisms of the "free market." They are pursuing quality of life and they are well aware that sustainability is not only a mission to protect the land

and our future, but also an added value that can make a farming economy attractive and gratifying.

The development of the Slow Food youth network provides further reassurance that all the work we have done so far to restore dignity to agriculture is bearing its first fruits. Young consumers are being guided in their choices by a new form of gastronomic sensitivity, and they are so passionate about food and agriculture that even we of the older generations, whose job it is to follow and support them, have much to learn from their enthusiasm and creativity. This has been my experience with the students at Pollenzo and the youngsters I meet regularly across the Slow Food and Terra Madre network at every latitude.

Women, old people, and young people—guardians of our future insofar as they, too, are factors in the explosion of diversity. They are like enzymes, ferments, and antibodies for our global society, capable of making it change, progress, improve, and heal. They are anything but outcasts, anything but the "fifth wheel of the wagon." They liberate positive energy and they are the human face of biodiversity. Then there are indigenous peoples . . .

# CHAPTER 9

# INDIGENOUS PEOPLES

"Out of 10,000 vegetable species suitable for human consumption, we commercialize 150. And if these 150 species contribute to 60 percent of human food consumption, what happens to the other 9,850? They are the food of indigenous peoples. I believe that the problem of food sovereignty is, first and foremost, a problem of food identity." These words, pronounced by my friend José Esquinas-Alcazar, director of CEHAP (Catedra de Estudios sobre Hambre y Pobreza) at the University of Cordoba, and for thirty years engaged in defending biodiversity at FAO, were the ones that struck me most at a conference on "Indigenous peoples and local food sovereignty" during the last Salone del Gusto–Terra Madre event in Turin in 2012.

José's was one of those perfect utterances that manage to elucidate a huge problem—in this case, the defense of world biodiversity—with a handful of simple figures. We tend to think of indigenous peoples as backward, yet it is they who fearlessly continue, against silence, indifference, prejudice, and injustice, to steward portions of land on which they have lived since time immemorial, in harmony with creation, of which they have an ever-enthralling cosmogonic vision.

Slow Food's empathy with indigenous peoples is total. It is within Terra Madre that the international debate has developed, and through its network that these peoples have forged contacts and initiatives to share their problems and assert their self-determination, recognized as a right by the Universal Declaration on the Rights of Indigenous Peoples adopted by the General Assembly of the UN in 2007.

Yet all this is still not enough. In 2011, we organized the first Terra Madre Indigenous People event in Sweden, in the lands of the Sami people—better known as Laps, but in Swedish this is a disparaging term. In 2014, the event will be staged again, this time in India, the country where I first grasped just how urgent and pivotal the indigenous question is for the whole planet. The richness of the thirty tribal communities I visited in northern India in 2010 left an indelible impression on me. A couple of thousand people had gathered to discuss their affairs, to show off their traditions and recipes, to listen to the devisers of Terra Madre, which they knew about because their representatives had been to Turin, a place, at once real and virtual, which they evidently regard as perfect for presenting their demands to the international or national agencies that ought to be protecting them. Their food was wonderful, mouthwateringly delicious, unbelievably varied. On that visit, I was also struck by the range of languages spoken and the complicated system of consecutive translations these people used to communicate among themselves. It was a moving encounter, as were the ones I have had with Brazilian, Australian, African, and North American indigenous peoples. These encounters have always gifted me something and given me the clear sensation that the world is adopting the wrong approach.

Indigenous peoples were, obviously, the leading players at the Terra Madre event dedicated to them in 2010. On that occasion, six of their representatives, one per continent, celebrated the official inauguration ceremony in front of the plenary assembly of all the food communities from 150 countries, and they dazzled the floor with their words and their traditional costumes. Let me report the exact words of Adolfo Timótio, better known as "Verá Mirim" of the Guarani Mbya people in Brazil:

First of all, I wish to thank Nhanderu, our Supreme Father, who has allowed me to be here today with all my strength and in good health. Five hundred and eighteen years after the Spanish invasion of the American continent, here I am to say that Nhanderu has illuminated us and guided us, and following his light we have been able to come through the whole process of colonization, fighting against slavery, for the right to our land, for the right to keep our language, our religion and our traditions. And we have come here to say that we are alive, that we haven't been destroyed, that our culture and our people are still standing [ . . . ]

I am the chief of my community in the indigenous land of Riberão Silveira in the State of São Paulo. I am also a producer and coordinator of the Slow Food Juçara Palm Heart Presidium. Today there are 40,000 Guarani and they live in areas of south, southeast, and central-west Brazil, in Paraguay, Argentina, and Bolivia. This was our territory until the Portuguese and Spanish arrived in South America. It wasn't we who created the frontiers. But in Brazil, where I come from, there were over a thousand indigenous populations and five million indigenous people. All this changed with the invasion. We lost our territories, our men and women were made slaves or died in battle, or of diseases previously unknown to us.

In Brazil, of the thousand indigenous groups who lived there only 229 remain. The five million indigenous inhabitants have now been reduced to 800,000.

With the end of colonization, we had to go on fighting against the holders of political and economic power to keep the right to live as different peoples [ . . . ]

We are all sacred beings. The Earth is sacred. It is our mother. This is why we respect Nature. Every time we take something from the forest for our survival—be it wood or a fruit or an animal—we first ask the permission of the spirits that protect the beings that live in the forest. We also respect the right moment for planting and hunting and cutting wood.

Everybody says that the Earth is sick. That natural resources are coming to an end. They talk about global warming that threatens to destroy life on the planet. We know that the forms of economic production that predominate in the world are the root cause of all this. During their religious rituals, our shamans always used to speak about the tragedy that is hitting the Earth today. They predicted that the World would fall ill, that it would be destroyed by the white man a little at a time. It wouldn't be God who destroyed the Earth.

We must join together to say that there are other ways of relating to Nature and to other human beings; that we can have access to the resources of the Earth without destroying it; that there are fairer and more sustainable ways of organizing human societies, in which justice, equality, and respect among different people and cultures prevail. In which differences are accepted and respected by everyone.

There is a scene at the end of my book *Slow Food Nation* that I recall as the embodiment of happiness. Invited to the San Carlo Theater in Naples to receive a Slow Food Award for Biodiversity in 2003, Getúlio Orlando Pinto Krahô, the chief of the Krahô community in the Brazilian state of Tocantins, ended his acceptance speech by singing a sacred song to thank us and tell us he was happy. On the stage on which Caruso had once performed, in front of an audience from all over the world, his singing moved all those present in a way that is impossible to describe. Adolfo Timótio also ended his Terra Madre speech with a song, one of those tribal chants that, he said, "gives our community spiritual strength." I have to admit that as I watched and listened, paralyzed by emotion, it gave me strength, too.

Today indigenous peoples play a big part in the Slow Food and Terra Madre movement, giving it an extra, irreplaceable injection of diversity, hence of creativity. To represent them, we have chosen Phrang Roy, coordinator of the Indigenous Partnership for Agrobiodiversity and Food Sovereignty. He is an internationally recognized expert on rural development, gender issues, and indigenous peoples. The Partnership coordinates and brings together communities pledged to defending their right to food and the promotion of sustainable environmental practices, in close collaboration with researchers and experts—and Slow Food—who share its principles. Phrang, who was my guide on that 2010 journey around India, was recently elected a member of the Slow Food International Council after the last Congress in Turin. To liberate diversity, we need indigenous peoples, their inspiration and their skill sets and learning on the right to food, food sovereignty, biodiversity protection, and sustainability.

Though a speech I delivered to the Permanent Forum of the UN on indigenous questions received little media coverage, I am not particularly dismayed. But I do think the fact that I was the first member of civil society not belonging to one of the indigenous peoples to be invited to speak there was one of the greatest recognitions I have ever received for my twenty years' work on food freedom. An old Native American saying goes like this: "Teach your children what we have taught our children, that the earth is our mother. Whatever befalls the earth, befalls the sons of the earth. If men spit upon the ground, they spit upon themselves . . . The Earth does not belong to man;

man belongs to Earth . . . The Earth is worth more than money and will last forever."

All humanity is indebted to indigenous peoples, who kept these principles alive in their daily practices while the world was going in a completely different direction.

# CHAPTER 10
# TOOLS

I f you look for the word "liberation" in the dictionary, one of the definitions will refer to its use in chemistry and physics. The liberation of energy is "release as a result of chemical reaction or physical decomposition." Diversity is our tool for releasing energy and making it available to the world so the world can change. Which is why we decided to embody it fully in the Slow Food that emerged from its 2012 congress. In the association's management bodies, which previously had been chosen in proportion to the number of each country's members, we decided to open up to quality as well as quantity. This is how people like Helianti Hilman, Phrang, and many others from Africa and South America, who I shall introduce later, were nominated. These are all people we met and began working with thanks to the advent of Terra Madre. They do not bring us new members—we cannot impose the idea of traditional Western associationalism on the whole world—but they do bring the humanity and fertility of their communities.

Change may have taken a long time, decades, in fact, but it always comes eventually if you trust in diversity. Now there is no turning back and change sometimes risks overtaking us. This is what the journey embarked upon in the Langa hills thirty years ago has made us: it has allowed us to embrace all the faces, all the skills, all the foods, all the visions of existence that our friends on every continent bring. Believe me, getting to know these people in the course of time, seeing them in their own homelands, then all together at events, is something that takes the breath away and makes the imagination fly. It makes one think what the earth and its principal fruit, food, would be if only everyone allowed this energy to be released, if standardization, waste, and "free market" were to be replaced by respect, exchange, or even only curiosity. I am confident that diversity will come out on top because there is no way of stopping it. It is already winning.

I have told a number of stories about Brazil in this chapter because Brazil is paradigmatic for my argument. In a blog article on July 30, 2013, my friend, the internationally renowned sociologist Domenico De Masi, wrote about Pope Francis's historic visit to Rio de Janeiro, where he was greeted by huge crowds. Just a fortnight earlier, the same crowds had demonstrated against government corruption and social policies. The Pope, nonconformist as ever, surprised everyone with symbolic gestures and his often unorthodox words. There is something about De Masi's article that brings to mind the story of Cravero, the Bra missionary in Brazil:

> Whatever happens in Brazil, even the arrival of a brand new Pope, it's always Brazil that wins. That's what happened with the Portuguese, and that's what happened with the Americans. Anthropologists call it syncretism. What it really is is the victory of a centuries-old culture of hospitality, happiness, and eroticism. As a Jesuit, the Pope was likely expecting to win back Brazil, as an Argentine, used

to the tango, he was likely expecting to tame the erotic kick of the samba.

But the reality is that in a couple of weeks the movement of young Brazilians beat the institutions 2-0. It did President Dilma out of 20 percentage points in the popularity ratings by preventing her from eating her words over transport costs, while on the Pope it imposed "Brazilianess" which, far from having anything mystical or liturgical or religious about it, is always pure-state paganism, the victory of body over soul, of polytheism over monotheism. As the Caetano Veloso song goes, "*Não existe pecado a lado de baixo do equador*" (There is no sin under the equator), so there's no confession and no confessor either.

Diversity, the victory of "poly" over "mono," is changing the world faster than we would have ever imagined. We thus draw sustenance from it and harness it. But if it is to express its full potential, as if it were fuel in an engine, we also need to maintain the engine, namely the network, global or local, virtual or real. This is the other tool of liberation: a free network.

# III. A FREE NETWORK

## CHAPTER I

# TAKSIM

The first meeting of the new Slow Food International Council, elected at the 2012 Congress, marked a greater turning point than we had expected. It took place in Istanbul on June 15–16, 2013, during the long, hot days of protest in Taksim Square and Gezi Park, days of undeniably historic significance for Turkey. The new forty or so Slow Food International Council members from every continent were nearly all there, and together they formed the image we wanted this extended management body to have. Lining up for the first time alongside the countries with the most members—namely Italy, the USA, and Germany—there were other "minor" but strategic ones, Terra Madre communities, young members, spokespeople for indigenous groups. Diversity and creativity were what we were after and, thanks to the hope-raising speeches and stories of these new protagonists, the Istanbul meeting did not disappoint us. But even as the

meeting was marking a turnaround for the Slow Food movement, other events were happening around us of which we
were subsequently lucky enough to be eyewitnesses.

Most of the preparatory organization of the meeting had been
done by members of the Slow Food staff in Bra, who also came
to Istanbul, and by our Turkish convivia, especially those in the
city itself. We were their guests and they did their job unforgetta-
bly well. They explained to us Turkey's gastronomic traditions—a
melting pot of influences, faraway in space and time—and treated
us to some of their dishes. They taught us about the biodiversity of a country that, if ever it were to close its borders, would
be perfectly capable of feeding itself. Turkey's diversity of environments, climates, and cultural influences produce foods of
every type and for every need. Before we got down to the two
days of work and meetings that lay ahead of us. Defne Koryürek,
the hyper-active Istanbul convivium leader and member of the
International Council for Turkey, gave us a briefing.

We had all gathered together in a large room on the top floor of
the headquarters of Salt, a cultural foundation in the Galata quarter in the old town. From the panoramic windows we could see
the Galata Bridge, nicknamed Europe's "optic nerve," and, in all
its magnificence, the skyline of what used to be Constantinople.

It was against this backdrop that Defne stood up and, after
having the lights dimmed, screened a video posted on You-
Tube. In it a handheld camera showed the demonstrators being
cleared out of Taksim Square for the first time. They had been
protesting for some days against the cutting down of trees and
the demolition of the adjacent Gezi Park, the only green area
left in the neighborhood, to make room for a large new shopping center (presented as a "cultural" center by the property
speculators). The violence used by the police against the demonstrators needs little comment from me, as it was broadcast
on every TV news program in the world for days after. The

police reaction was over the top right from the start. A young woman who had been invited up by Defne, and who had been present at the first removal of the protesters that we had seen in the video, told us she had gone to the park on the eve of the planned cutting-down to "bid farewell to her trees," simply because that was her park, the place she had gone to walk in ever since childhood. She had had no intention of demonstrating, she just wanted to say "good-bye" and to meditate. There were maybe a dozen tents belonging to the activists who intended to stand up to the cutting down of the trees at all costs, but most of the hundred or so people present were simply lovers of the park and happened to be there without prior agreement. The police mowed them down without a modicum of civil respect, injuring many with their batons and their tear gas. The day after, as soon as news of the violent removal spread, a couple of thousand people swarmed into Taksim Square and the number mounted night by night, many inhabitants of Istanbul going there straight after work. Clashes with the police became the norm, as did police violence. There was no shortage of casualties, some of them serious, and, alas, fatalities.

Defne calmly explained to us what the situation had been like in Gezi Park up to then—it was the Saturday morning—and told us that the younger members of the Istanbul Slow Food convivium, the vast majority of whom were teenagers, among them her daughter, had been going there every day and some even slept there overnight. After the removal she had told us about, the demonstration had been spontaneously organized, with thousands of people occupying the park permanently, setting up field hospitals and kitchen tents that served up free food for everyone there, among them entire families. Slow Food youngsters and others had even tried to plant a garden near the trees. Every night concerts and film shows and artistic events were staged, some of them of a certain prestige and involving important major celebrities.

Turkey, the bridge between Europe and Asia, is made up, on the one hand, of young people who look toward Europe and new paradigms and lifestyles, and, on the other, by the slight Asian Muslim majority that elected president Recep Tayyip Erdogan, the main instigator of the heavy-handedness against the demonstrators. Many people in Istanbul were quick to join the demonstrations against Erdogan, a premier who has given impressive impetus to the Turkish economy—partly thanks to aggressive, unecological policies that have led, among other things, to overbuilding—but he has also introduced measures to limit personal freedom, thus fomenting the fundamentalist itch of the many Muslims who support him. Hence restrictions on the sale of alcohol and the opening times of bars and clubs, bans on kissing in public, control of the Internet—all actions that have hit hard at the lives of youngsters who, with their ways of enjoying themselves and communicating and being together, have created a new cosmopolitan atmosphere in Istanbul. One has the immediate impression of a city in frenetic motion that is changing in front of one's eyes, full of construction sites and industry, but also of enthusiasm and innovation. Here Asia and Europe meet geographically and stare at each other, as old and new progress fuses into a unique, high-speed evolution, apparently uncontrollable, still less fully fathomable.

Street protests were also recorded in Ankara, the capital, and Smyrna, where more young people died. The situation was slipping out of Erdogan's grasp. Not that he was ever prepared to see reason; on the contrary, he subsequently stepped up the repression. On the Saturday evening, June 15, we, the whole International Council, were supposed to go for dinner in a large private house with a spectacular terrace, not far from Taksim Square. The meal was to be prepared by the brilliant Semsa Denizsel, chef at Kantin, a restaurant where the food draws on various traditions from different parts of Turkey and uses lots of local ingredients, many of which are grown nearby. The news that was reaching us was, alas, anything but reassuring. Erdogan was coming back to town after a trip abroad and a rumor was going around that he intended to take strong action against the people occupying Taksim Square, that he had organized a huge rally with his own supporters for the following day. His target, it was said, was a turnout of a million. Defne and the young women of the convivium were reluctant to expose the members of the International Board to scenes of urban guerilla warfare, and for safety reasons they decided, at the last minute, to switch the dinner venue to Kantin, Semsa Denizsel's restaurant. There would not be seating room for everyone, but we could make the evening into a more informal—and safer—affair and still enjoy the menu Semsa had planned for us.

We went to the restaurant by bus and everything seemed quiet enough. True, the city was living a moment of extreme tension, but away from the "hot" zone you could hardly tell. Life seemed to be going on as normal, as frenetically as ever. It was only exchanging a few words with taxi drivers, hearing the opinions of hotel staff, shopkeepers, and restaurant owners that you got some inkling of what was happening. As I say, everything seemed confined to a single neighborhood.

The traffic was light and we got to Kantin on time. We sat around, some of us on the veranda, some in the garden, others in the two large dining rooms: aperitifs, the first few dishes on the menu, good wines. At a certain point, the young women and the restaurant staff started making phone calls, sending text messages, muttering among themselves, and going onto the Internet with their mobiles. The police had waded into the crowd in Gezi Park again, more violently and systematically than the first time, using water hydrants (which we were later to find out contained irritants diluted with the water), tear gas, and stinging gas, spraying them at eye level at women, children, and the elderly—at all the humanity who happened to be there, even locals who had just popped out for their evening constitutional. Contravening all Defne's instructions, I had been in the park the day before, and I had seen the garden and spoken to groups of protesters. Some Italian Slow Food people intended to go there that night after the dinner. There had been a lot of people in the park, and after the police intervention, they had dispersed into the surrounding streets, some of them as far as the restaurant where we were dining. We were looking down into the street when cars started speeding by sounding their horns. Then the demonstrators, recognizable by their headscarves, eye masks, hard hats, and protective goggles, came running up. There were just a few of them at first, but soon a whole mass of them appeared, followed by the pungent smell of tear gas. A stone's throw from the restaurant, a barricade was erected on the main boulevard, and Defne literally locked us up inside the restaurant, refusing to let us leave. It could have been very dangerous indeed to get mixed up in the trouble and overwhelmed by the fury of the police. It has to be said that the demonstrators' methods—passive resistance, self-defense, advancing only whenever the police withdrew—were entirely peaceful.

Back at the restaurant we were all slightly taken aback. More than anything else, we were worried about the Turkish teenagers, some of the youngest of whom were visibly upset because many of their friends had been in the crowd in Gezi Park. We were all warned not to tweet or use Facebook for fear that the police would be able to trace our messages; after all, people had already been arrested in Istanbul for tweets on the Internet. All those present watched impotently through a large window as the demonstrators trickled away off the main street that ran down into Taksim Square, a couple of kilometers away. In the meantime, dishes were still being served from the kitchen, and they were getting better and better, more and more complex. Not that everybody was eating at this point. Food was being left on the well-laid tables and the whole scene had something "Fellinian" about it, something dreamlike and surreal. I couldn't help thinking of Mao Zedong's famous phrase, "Revolution isn't a dinner party." No, it wasn't, and maybe it wasn't right for us to stay in the restaurant. But we were blocked there and the roads were blocked, too, and what with the barricades and the police presence, taxi cabs, still less our buses, were unable to circulate in the area.

It was Semsa Denizsel who spared us our embarrassment when she came out of the kitchen with a huge tray of steamed ravioli stuffed with lamb, a syncretic dish suspended midway between East and West, partly reminiscent of Chinese dim sum, partly of European stuffed pasta. Semsa the chef smiled and said:

> Turkey is being liberated, this is a struggle for our civil rights, and I'm happy you're here in my restaurant at this moment in time. I'm happy because, when you go home, you'll talk about it, and this you have to do with as many people as you can. But please don't stop eating because I'm not going to stop cooking! At this moment, it's the only thing we can do to help, even if indirectly, those people down in the street. Staying together and enjoying our gastronomic traditions together, sharing to the full an experience that is going to change us—all of us—at least a little. Keep eating, please. It's our way of saying that we're here, that we aren't afraid, that we're building our future.

A thunderous round of applause rang around the restaurant and the Turkish young women—not to mention one or two collaborators from Bra—struggled to hide their heartfelt emotion. We ended the dinner a little calmer than we started it. A couple of hours later in a street littered with wrecked barricades, as we sought with some difficulty to hail a taxi back to our hotels and the clashes seemed to have died down, I thought, "Maybe Mao was wrong, maybe revolution can be a table set for dinner, be it real or metaphorical."

# CHAPTER 2

# FROM ISTANBUL TO SEATTLE WITH STOPS ALONG THE WAY

The following day, we resumed our meeting. When it ended, on schedule, at one o'clock, we were walking back to our hotels when we heard chanting in the distance. My hotel was on a block in front of the Galata Bridge between two streets that ran up into Taksim Square. A mass of humanity was marching up them: many youngsters, whole families with babies and children, a lot of old people, and also women with veils. Almost all of them were wearing handkerchiefs or masks across their faces, goggles, and hard hats. For anyone without this basic protection gear, impromptu vendors were selling all sorts of items, as well as fruit and water. The city was mobilizing, but not only in one direction. Buses taking people to the scheduled pro-Erdogan demonstration out in the suburbs were going past the hotel. These were Erdogan's supporters, but apparently they included every civil servant in Istanbul, all "obliged" to go. The demonstration turned out to be colossal and effectively did draw a million people. But hundreds of thousands of others were also coming in from all over the city, some crossing the bridges on foot from the farthest neighborhoods on the Asian coast. The night before, when the news spread of the clearing of Gezi Park, 40,000 people had walked across the main bridge over the Bosporus. As one commentator put it, "If 40,000 people walk from one continent to another, it means something historic is happening."

We spent hours watching that colorful stream of determined but also cheerful people. The families looked as if they were on a Sunday outing. Everyone was very calm, only chanting occasionally or booing when the buses carrying Erdogan's supporters drove past with their orange flags. The maître d'hôtel, a young man, pointed at the folks walking up to Taksim Square. "Look at them," he asked me. "Do they look like terrorists to you?" That was how the premier had described them. Half an hour later, the maître d' mounted his scooter and set off for the square himself.

Toward six o'clock, the crowd started coming back down again, moving faster and faster. In the space of a few minutes, they built a huge barricade across the boulevard in front of my hotel. In a flash we were being showered with tear gas and the effects were very painful. We took shelter inside the hotel and asked for lemons to relieve the burning sensation, but it was still impossible to breathe. Eventually they opened the roof terrace and we were able to regain our breath at last. We were also able to get an aerial view of the clashes, which went on for hours and hours. Around midnight, the scoops were already removing the debris from the streets and everything seemed to be over. The next morning, we managed to get to the airport without further ado; in the meantime, the city appeared to have resumed its usual relentless rhythm. But that was not the end of the problems, which still exist as I write. Ways of protesting and opposing the Erdogan government may have changed, but the misdemeanors and repression of the police are continuing by other means. Since June 2013, Gezi Park has been rebuilt and the construction of the planned shopping center, or cultural center as they call it, has been postponed until who knows when. Nothing is certain yet, but two months after the events I have described, people were still meeting in Gezi Park every night. Defne tells me the place now appears somewhat artificial and "gentrified," but the true victory for the locals is the fact that they can still get out of their houses to talk. The same thing is beginning to happen in other green spaces in the city. Every two days there are skirmishes with the police, who refuse to tolerate public gatherings. Some clashes are more violent than others, but in the meantime the protests have liberated a new energy, and all over the city people meet after work to talk, to get to know each other, to swap opinions, and even to eat together. There are gardens, people having picnics, small farmers' markets. Istanbul and its inhabitants are no longer the same after the events of Gezi Park and Taksim Square.

There we witnessed a clash of civilizations and a revolution. Whether it was big or small, only history will tell. Those confrontations were, above all, an expression of worlds colliding, of different visions, of change that cannot be stopped or repressed. Now, perhaps, a dialogue is underway. There is still a lot of uncertainty, which is inevitable, but the climate is more fertile than ever, and Erdogan has promised to protect a vast green area out in the suburbs on the road to the airport, to turn it into Istanbul's answer to Central Park. Which means that even the government may have gotten the message.

Two weeks after the events in Turkey, more much-publicized riots broke out in Rio during the Confederations Cup soccer tournament. The root cause was an increase in bus fares, but soon the whole thing turned into an enormous street demonstration against the government of Dilma Rousseff, president in the post-Lula years. In Brazil, too, there were deaths and casualties and ruthless repression in all the cities in which demonstrations flared up. It is no coincidence that the events in Turkey and Brazil were somehow interlinked. Here are two of the countries with the highest rates of economic development in the world, but in neither does the whole population benefit from that development. Over the last few years, the *Fome zero* (Zero Hunger) campaign, launched by president Lula and successfully implemented by José Graziano da Silva, then a minister, now director general of the Food and Agriculture Organization, has solved the age-old problem of hunger and malnutrition in Brazil. They have done a good job, but the campaign was a beginning, not an end. Development brings well-being and, with it, other needs, accompanied by demands for other rights. I thought back to Italy in the postwar years and the 1960s, to the miracle of the economic boom, to the violent repression of those years. We in Italy have seen scenes like the ones in Turkey and Brazil before, but maybe we have forgotten about them.

They are scenes that are recurring with increasing frequency around the world, in all societies and in every type of situation. The causes may change and the triggers may change, but they all have a common denominator: namely the demand, especially on the part of the young generations, for a new development model to govern and manage the delicate ecological and social questions that are coming to the fore in this period in history, defined as postmodern. It is hard to generalize without trivializing individual protests and situations, but since the anti-globalization protest in Seattle during the World Trade Organization meeting in 1999, cases have certainly multiplied with growing frequency. Considering the last few years alone, the following come to mind: the "Arab Spring" that spread over most of North Africa (the last Slow Food International Council meeting prior to the 2012 congress actually took place in Morocco in the middle of the unrest, but went off without incident); the Occupy movement in New York City's Zuccotti Park, which gave a political shock to a United States in the throes of economic crisis; the peaceful mobilization of the Indignados, which began in Spain in 2011 and fanned out across the world to promote greater collective participation in democratic life and political and economic decisions. I would also add the "NO TAV" protests in the Susa Valley, very near Bra, which, as I write, have by no means died out.[20] Leaving aside its rights and wrongs, the dispute represents a proud defense of the integrity of a local area, involving people of every generation and every social class. Though the demonstrators tend to be portrayed as "terrorists"—this was the case in Turkey—they have almost always conducted their protests in a very civilized fashion.

From the observation point of an international network like Slow Food and Terra Madre, I cannot help noticing how all these movements intersect. They may not be fully and mutually sympathetic, but they come close. I say this because they have contacts with and touch the Slow Food world more or less directly.

At least judging by the ideas and issues that hold it together, Terra Madre is a network that has exerted a certain influence. I have already spoken about the youngsters of Slow Food Istanbul and the garden in Gezi Park. Later we shall see what is happening in the favelas of Brazil, how the Maghreb has responded with

[20] A reference to the ongoing protests against the building of the Turin-Lyon high-speed railroad through the Susa Valley in western Piedmont. TAV is the Italian acronym for *Treno ad alta velocità*, high-speed train.

a number of cooperation movements, and how, in Italy, too, the protection of the landscape and common goods will depend on new networks connecting, integrating, and joining together. Today there is already a new way of building the future that unites a variety of sentiments and causes—which, until a few years ago, appeared lost or unimportant—now broadly shared, especially by the new generations, and capable of cutting across populations, geographically and generationally—even, I might add, ideologically. A common feeling is sweeping the world, the "good, clean, and fair" world. What is certain is that all the people I mention are fighting for self-determination, for quality of life, for social justice and ecology, for the sustainability of human processes. They often attribute a central role to food or include it in their struggles, and their protests display a novel dynamic that we now have to master as a new paradigm. I am referring to the swarm mechanism, beautifully explained by Zygmunt Bauman in his brief and enlightening essay *Does Ethics Have a Chance in a World of Consumers* (Harvard University Press, 2009):

> . . . we can note another striking similarity between the way the wasps of Panama live and the way we live. In a liquid-modern society, *swarms* tend to replace *groups*, with their leaders, hierarchies, and pecking orders. A swarm can do without all those paraphernalia without which a group could not exist. Swarms need not be burdened by the group's tools of survival; they assemble, disperse, and come together again from one occasion to another, each time guided by different, invariably shifting relevancies, and attracted by shifting and moving targets. The seductive pull of shifting targets is a rule sufficient to coordinate the swarm's movements—and so commands or other forms of enforcement "from the top" are redundant (in fact the "top" itself—the center—is redundant): A swarm has no top, no center; it is solely the direction of its current flight that casts some of the self-propelled swarm units into the

position of "leaders" to be followed for the duration of a particular flight or a part of it, though hardly longer.

We are living in an age of swarms.

Swarms feed on meetings and communication through networks, "liquid networks." Which is precisely why, after liberated diversity, these networks are our second indispensable tool. What is needed is a free network, a physical and virtual place in which "everything [that] has begun again"[21] can continue and sustain itself and spread. A place of free exchange (and I mean free!), of experiences and values and identities, a place of new gastronomy and new politics, the infrastructure of a diversity—and diversities—yet to be waylaid by politics, but which is already political. It is necessary to interact with these subjects, these swarms, playing an active part and making a contribution by pointing them in new directions. It is necessary to understand the members and the needs of this humanity that is asking the world to change, to make its stories and ideas bear fruit. I would even go as far as to say that our specificity—I am referring to the Slow Food association—needs almost to melt inside this network and mingle with the swarms, free to follow new directions according to circumstance. I would have no fear of going through with this, a process that would be liberating for any structure. For no structure on its own can ever represent the complexity of the world.

---

[21] See page 36, note 6.

# CHAPTER 3

# TEN THOUSAND NODES IN THE FREE NETWORK

We now come to the second of the "three ten thousands" mentioned previously. After loading ten thousand food products onto the Ark of Taste to set free diversity, the next main target is to add ten thousand nodes to our network, ten thousand points of vitality that will fit into the broader network of global change and animate it with good practices. But the network has to be free.

At Slow Food we really got down to thinking about this "liquid" form of organization, the network, immediately after the first Terra Madre event in 2004. On that occasion we succeeded in bringing to Turin more than 6,000 people representing about 1,200 food communities from more than 150 different countries. We had passed the first difficult test we had set ourselves. The mega meeting, the travel, the complicated organization with all its problems of logistics—everything had run smoothly without major setbacks. Even the outcome had exceeded our expectations, as, deep down, we had hoped it would. Any questions about what we should do next were answered by the communities themselves, even before we had the time to ask them. After a few months, we realized that other informal networks—of indigenous peoples, of nomadic peoples, of small-scale fishers, of shepherds—had already been formed through contacts and exchanges among the communities. After meeting in Turin, people sharing the same problems from different parts of the world were tending to join together, to keep in touch, to swap experiences, solutions, and ideas. At the request of the communities at the grassroots level, regional, national, and continental Terra Madre meetings were organized in Scandinavia, Brazil, Argentina, Africa, Australia, the Balkans, and South Korea, as well as among indigenous peoples. We then instituted Terra Madre Day, which is now held every year on December 10, when all the food communities get together and stage a small event, a celebration, or a meeting in their local areas. Every year well-nigh 1,000 initiatives are held simultaneously on Slow Food Day to create a sense of a present, active world network.

Driven by sentiments that I call "affective intelligence" (the cement of the network laid by fraternity and the exercise of less logical, more human intelligence) and "austere anarchy" (no one tells the communities or the nodes what to do in detail, how to organize themselves or how to work), this free network was beginning to show a certain dissonance from what Slow Food had been until that moment. The majority of Terra Madre communities were and are not formally a part of the association. In other words, the people who combine to form them were not and are not Slow Food members. Slow Food was and is the organizer of the Terra Madre meetings, the spark that set the network on fire. In its institutional form, the association was not and never will be ready to represent internally the complexity of the Terra Madre communities, many of which come from cultural realities that do not even conceive of associationalism as we know it and of which we boast a long tradition. Paradoxical situations have been recorded in the last ten years, but fortunately the ideal adherence of all concerned—be they Slow Food membership card holders or food communities—has allowed us to overcome problems of form and keep the network united, even triggering unhoped-for phenomena. In places in which Slow Food was not even present—many parts of Africa, South America, and Asia—its snail was immediately identified with Terra Madre and seen as a symbol to relate to. Which is why Slow Food flags fly in the courtyards of Lare and why the restaurant of the women of the local Pumpkin Presidium is called Slow Food Hotel. The same is happening in hundreds of other places, which Slow Food might never have reached, but where it is now effectively present. All the African members of the Slow Food International Council, for example, come from Terra Madre, indeed discovered Slow Food through Terra Madre.

To erase these dissonances, in 2012 we decided to make the Salone del Gusto and Terra Madre a single event—previously they had been held simultaneously, but the fact that they tended to occupy different spaces made them feel separate—opening their doors to each other and mixing their respective diversities. This was a powerful signal. The International Congress that was held at the same time knocked down every barrier—even the most formal—by decreeing once and for all the entry of the Terra Madre communities into Slow Food's management bodies, even though they do not carry the same cardholding weight as the convivia, the local nodes of the world network. This was the result of a slow process that is still underway today, almost ten years since the first Terra Madre event. In short, October 2012 saw the birth of Slow Food 2.0, a new version of the movement, more "liquid," much vaster than a simple association. Now there is no going back.

This is why we decided to "unpair the cards" by setting ourselves the target of 10,000 nodes on the network. It is a mistake to rest on one's laurels; liberation can only be pursued by upping the ante. Today the Slow Food association has about 100,000 fully paid-up members around the world organized into about 1,500 convivia—trifling figures compared to all the humanity that gravitates around it or is connected with it. There are 2,000 Terra Madre communities, 400 Presidia with all their producers, 700 educational projects involving children and teachers in schools, an alliance of 1,700 cooks and chefs with their restaurants, 1,000 school and community gardens in Africa, and the Slow Food Youth Network, whose youngsters are not always members but participate more informally. Then there are the indigenous peoples, whose "parliament" during my visit to the UN recognized Slow Food as their only non-institutional partner in civil society. Just think of the number of people involved: it would not be excessive to imagine a figure somewhere in the region of 600,000 to a million.

The existing network is thus growing in size, and this is why, in parallel with our 10,000-node target, we also performed a more specific internal census to get a better idea of who we are and how many of us there are. For the energies liberated by Terra Madre are hard to control, hence to quantify. But one thing for sure is that they are immense. It is impossible to predict which directions they will flow in and we have no intention of "commanding" or orienting these processes "from the top," of sticking labels or planting flags on the network. Since we stopped contemplating our navel and gave life to Terra Madre, this huge, liberating change has been set in motion internally. Not that we intend to contemplate our new navel—the solid reality of food communities in more than 170 countries around the world—

either. The problem is not one of governance, but of implementing and driving flows of energy through the nodes of the network. The network is free and free it must remain. We simply want to have a better idea of who we are and support the most deserving projects. And we want the world to talk about us and to intersect other networks more than we are doing at the moment. We want to transfuse our ideas—"liberated" gastronomy—and our force—unbound diversity multiplied to the umpteenth degree—to forge new and undreamed-of exchanges.

The project seems to have worked to date, and expanding its scope can only lead to interesting novelties and paradigms capable of grasping the things that politics is ignoring, such as the demands of the young people who take to the streets to claim their freedom. Maybe we thought the time for invoking *liberté, egalité et fraternité* was over. But what with the revolutions, great and small, that are happening in the world every day—though we may not notice them or witness them firsthand without being able to grasp their scope—the three concepts are as actual as they ever were.

Let us place our trust in them by continuing to implement free networks, bringers of human progress and rebirth. And let us do so not virtually—which is all the rage—but concretely. It is important to remember that the people of Terra Madre are not faraway entities interconnected by computer or telephone: they are flesh-and-blood human beings who work actively every day, who are devoted to local areas and local realities, but also have a greater, much greater, well-being at heart. This is the force of the Slow Food–Terra Madre free network: it is real and it is tangible.

## CHAPTER 4

# FOR EXAMPLE: A GREEN STAR ON A RED FIELD[22]

Here is a form submitted to the jury of the Slow Food Award for Biodiversity in 2001, the presentation ceremony of which was held in Oporto, in Portugal:

Name: COOPERATIVE AMAL DE TAMANAR
Nationality: Moroccan (Essaouira)
Field of activity: agriculture

Description:

The Coopérative Amal de Tamanar was formed in 1996 and inaugurated in 1999 (with the support of the British embassy in Morocco). It has 47 female members.

---

[22] Reference to the Moroccan national flag.

Objective:

The protection of *arganier* groves, the use of their fruits, and the promotion of traditional organic produce (the cooperative has received certification from the French national "Qualité" agency), such as edible argan oil, *amlou* and *arganium*. At the same time, the cooperative supports women in the Moroccan countryside.

Motivation for the proposal:

The *araganier* tree (*Argania spinosa*) is a member of the Sapotaceae family, a species that already existed in the Tertiary age. The plant is considered native to the arid and semi-arid zones of Morocco. The wood of the tree is used both in carpentry and as firewood. The fruit is used to produce an edible oil, while the leaves and waste provide excellent forage for livestock in this arid region.

Once the *arganier* woods stretched over vast tracts of the southwest Morocco—about 1,400,000 hectares—but now they cover fewer than 830,000 hectares.

The tree now risks disappearing on account of aridity and human intervention.

The conferring of the Slow Food Award on the Amal cooperative would:

· encourage this association of peasant women to persevere in their noble intent of using these fruits rationally and extracting an organic oil using craft methods

· confirm the praiseworthiness of the cooperative's initiative in protecting the *arganier* tree, a world vegetable heritage, by reforesting the *arganeraie* of Sous

· promulgate knowledge of this endangered tree, its by-products (such as the oil) and its nutritional and cosmetic properties.

Nominated by: Prof. Ahmed Elamrani
Nationality: Moroccan
Annexes: presentation + 7 photos

Every year we used to receive almost 200 nominations like this one from a network of observers that included university professors, gastronomy and cooking experts, as well as Slow Food members and convivium leaders all over the world. In 2001, the Moroccan cooperative was singled out by the jury, which had the job of whittling the nominations down to a short list of fifteen or so. In the summer of that year, Slow Food collaborators and journalists set out from Bra to visit the places where these champions of biodiversity worked, first to check that the nominations were accurate and that the activity described was actually being performed, then to write up and document the stories behind them, which were subsequently published in fascinating little booklets, now out of print. It was Terra Madre *in nuce*, though we didn't realize it at the time.

I have reproduced the Amal de Tamanar nomination form, a veritable historical document, to paint a small fresco of Morocco and show how a free network is capable of releasing the right energies. The story of the Essaouira cooperative is paradigmatic insofar as its efforts to protect the *arganier* woods by producing oil and cosmetics, and its social rehabilitation work, have enjoyed incredible success. Remember that the cooperative is made up exclusively of women, some of whom were disowned by their families for the most absurd reasons. In Islamic society, the woman's role can be complicated, and the social and economic "redemption" of the forty-seven women of the Amal de Tamanar cooperative was soon being reproduced elsewhere.

On my last trip to Morocco in 2011, I was able to see for myself how the argan seed, the fruit of these trees, is once more a very common resource in the southwest of the country. Argan oil is now appearing on all the most important tables of Europe and in wellness centers half the world over. A farming economy that was gradually disappearing has now made made a spectacular comeback thanks to the recovery of old techniques and crops, but in a very modern context with extensive use of new technologies, especially the Internet and social networks. After the 2001 award ceremony, some Ligurian oil producers close to the world of Slow Food joined with the Amal de Tamanar cooperative and organized exchange trips to teach the Moroccan women the best techniques for preserving and packaging their oil—the use of dark glass bottles, for example, to prevent it from oxidizing. This may sound like a minor detail, but the momentum it gave was such an impetus that, in that area of Morocco, 170 women's cooperatives are now processing argan oil, employing about 5,000 women. In other words, a small revolution.

In Morocco, a great collective effort of renewal has been underway for some years now, arguably more democratic and certainly more peaceful than in other North African contexts. King Mohammed VI is making a contribution with his modernization of the construction sector, placing the emphasis on the building of infrastructure. Agriculture still plays a preponderant role in the economy, employing more than 50 percent of the active population. The government is aiming to modernize this sector, too, but, unfortunately, most of its plans envisage intensive and industrial agriculture. Many Moroccan farms are still grounded in tradition and, rather than disrupting their characteristic activity, it might be advisable to adopt a third way like that of the women's cooperatives producing argan oil or the enterprises being developed by young people from the Terra Madre network. In 2011, I came across three of these in particular.

On that occasion I was taken to M'hamid El Ghizlane, a small town on the edge of the desert, no more than ten kilometers from the Algerian border. There Abdelouhab El Gasmi, his brother, and his mother have formed the Coopérative de l'Oasis du Sud, which, as the name says, is situated in an oasis. They process the dates they grow—a range of special native varieties—into a syrup known as *Rob* and into jams. They use recycled glass jars and market their products nationally and internationally, selling them through Facebook. Though they have to struggle with the problem of lack of water and are invaded by the red palm weevil, which can kill off date palms, they refuse to give up and, indeed, are constantly expanding their sales network. They have also managed to receive funding to buy drip-irrigation equipment and plant gardens for their community.

On the same journey I met Salahddine Sahrawi, a young agronomist from Safi, on the Atlantic coast. He is a member of the town's Forum d'Initiative Citoyen and works with many local grape, fig, and argan growers. He works hard at promoting these crops among cooks in towns and cities, and he travels to find new channels through which to commercialize them, such as farm shops and baskets of food for sale on the Internet—the network to the fore again.

Rachid El Hiyani, finally, works with saffron producers in Taliouine in the south of the country. He, too, intends to open boutiques to sell the products of his community and form cooperatives of small Moroccan producers. Such cooperatives are springing up like mushrooms in Morocco these days, partly thanks to the Ministry of the Economy's decision a few years ago to cut some of the red tape that used to hamper their development.

The people I have mentioned are all young and they use Facebook and Twitter, which were the main vehicles of communication and growth of the revolts of the so-called "Arab spring," which involved some of Morocco's neighbors a couple of years ago. They do so to keep themselves updated and in touch with one another, to exchange handy professional information, to sell their products directly as far afield as France and Germany. Even as "modern" farming and distribution techniques are taking hold in Morocco, based on the standardization and industrialization of processes, these youngsters believe in a different model, in biodiversity, and in the traditional wealth of their country. Much more "modernly," they are fixated on the sustainability of their techniques, which does not necessarily mean adhering to old models alone. Albeit respecting their communities' past and the needs of small farmers, they are innovating constantly.

Together with the women of the argan cooperatives, they are the most genuine face of a potential agricultural "spring." It is not utopian to imagine that in the future this may serve as a deterrent to the mass emigrations we have grown accustomed to, not only from Morocco but also from the rest of Africa. I repeat, something has already begun again, and this something uses the network to emerge and demonstrate, even in the most difficult, isolated areas, that the redemption of the land may be inspired by the common concern with sustainability, ecology, the protection of tradition, and biodiversity that is cutting across the whole world, while respecting the specific character of single places. Local is suddenly becoming global. Judging from the business being developed by the Terra Madre youngsters Abdelouhab El Gasmi, Salahddine Sahrawi, and Rachid El Hiyani, it is selling well, too.

## CHAPTER 5

# FROM A BELL IN NEW ORLEANS TO THE CROP MOBS OF DETROIT

In 1998 in New Orleans I had the honor of ringing the bell that sets trading in motion at the city's farmers' market. I was accompanied by Poppy Tucker, the local Slow Food convivium leader, at that time a member of the International Council. It is a wonderful old tradition: at the sound of the bell, shoppers flock around the stalls to buy the food farmers have brought in from the surrounding countryside, some from suburban or downtown urban farms. Bands strike up and the party atmosphere is immediately contagious. The freshest vegetables, raw milk cheese, craft beers, top-quality farm-butchered meat, bread and flatbreads, cakes, and bottles of fruit juice pass from hand to hand. It is a delicious way to spend a morning, shopping and occasionally nibbling local specialties, food produced within a radius of no more than 100 kilometers, all made with care and passion.

In 1998 all this was a whole new world for a visiting European. I recognized traces of ancient French and Italian market traditions, though in those days many of our neighborhood markets had grown "anemic," reduced to mere retail points for fruit and vegetables from central wholesale depots, with hardly any farmers or food producers present, no music (yes, I remember music being played at the markets in Bra), no eating in loco as one did one's shopping (with the exception of some of the historic southern Italian markets with their famous street food). In New Orleans I really was breathing in a new, fizzy atmosphere. "How come in America they have better markets than ours?" I wondered to myself. "We've got such a long tradition, yet the home of fast food has something to teach us." I really relished that morning spent meeting producers and hearing the wonderful tales they had to tell: their small rebellions against the frenetic society in which they were living, their passion for sustainability, the sacrality with which they handled their products. Single tomatoes, the precious fruits of hard but gratifying work, were pampered as if they were small babies—and they were outstanding. On my way home from New Orleans I stopped off in New York City, where I met brewmaster Garrett Oliver for the tour I described previously. There, bang in the middle of the Big Apple, I found the same infectious, relaxing spirit at the historic farmers' market in Union Square.

According to data published by the United States Department of Agriculture, at the time of my journey there were about 2,700 farmers' markets in the States, most of them in big cities. They heralded a small distributive revolution and new opportunities for organically minded farmers. They were manna from heaven for lovers of local food, hence the number of their customers was constantly on the up. In 2013, there were 8,100 of these markets and hundreds are being added to the list every year. In 1994, the first year the USDA made a census of them, there were 1,700. The states with the most farmers' markets are, in order, California (where my friend Alice Waters, longtime international vice-president of Slow Food, has been promoting organic and local food for over 40 years), New York, Michigan, Illinois, Ohio, and Pennsylvania. But the most significant recent increases, some as high as 30 percent a year, have been recorded in states such as Alaska, Texas, Colorado, and New Mexico, much less likely places than the two coasts, where cultural elites exert a strong, often pioneering influence. Having said this, and though their detractors are always complaining about their exorbitant prices, the markets are not elitist at all, and a great many of them accept the food stamps the government gives the needy to subsidize their food. Many of them are staged in city suburbs and draw producers and shoppers of every ethnic group and social class. In a market in Queens, in New York City, I noted how the Indian and Hispanic communities have "adopted" the market, not to mention how small farmers cater for them by learning to cultivate their favorite varieties and traditional food products.

Best of all, at the Queens market I met a family of immigrants from Mexico who had set up a farmstead just out of town with the support of the market organizers. They had thus been able to carry on the farm work they had been doing back home. They were fed up with making ends meet doing the tiring, alienating jobs so common among immigrants, the jobs native-born Americans are no longer prepared to do. They had found new prospects for a life that was better suited to them.

This type of market soon spread to Europe. For its part, Slow Food began organizing its so-called Earth Markets, part of a major, well-regulated international project inspired by the American model and by the Italian tradition in which producers sell only their own products. Milan and Bologna are the cities in which these markets have been most successful, attracting a network of informed consumers and circulating energies and projects, and, in some cases, giving youngsters the urge to return to the land. Other networks of markets subsequently grew up, the most important being Campagna Amica (Friendly Countryside), organized under the auspices of Coldiretti (the Italian National Farmers' Union), which is enjoying a certain amount of success in the principal Italian towns and cities, though it has less strict regulations than the markets organized by Slow Food. This is not a problem, however, given that the network offers diversity, nonetheless. Good ideas travel and it does not matter who puts them into practice. This is the principle that governs networks, after all; not only must it be accepted, it also needs to be spread.

Many of the participants in US farmers' markets are, needless to say, also members of the Terra Madre network and have been to Turin on at least one occasion. Over the years I have seen this movement grow to incredible levels in the United States, and today it is not only a matter of markets, but also of the farmers themselves. A 2010 meeting of the Georgia Organics Association in Athens, Georgia, convinced me of this once and for all. I had been invited to deliver a keynote speech at the meeting and I found myself speaking to an audience of 1,000 farmers from this enthralling southern state, all organic, all selling locally. "How many of you have been to Terra Madre at least once," I asked them. Much to my surprise about half their hands went up. The nice thing is that these farmers really do form a community. Besides being closely interconnected, they also develop direct relationships with city dwellers, supply the best restaurants, and forge contacts with the artistic, political, and educational worlds, plus others besides.

Then there is Community-Supported Agriculture, about which I have written extensively elsewhere, and which in the meantime has almost become the norm. A group of consumers allies with a farmer and asks how much the person intends to earn in a year with the food he or she produces. A total price is established and the group pays the full figure on the nail. Season by season, it is then up to the farmer to deliver a proportional amount of fresh local organic produce directly to the consumers' homes or to collection points, which are often to be found at farmers' markets. Consumers thus espouse the cause of farmers, protecting them from contingencies in return for certain fixed prices throughout the year. They share the risk, becoming what I call "co-producers," without getting their hands dirty. They are actively involved in the production process without producing anything directly. They see food consumption not as an action separate from production—even if only as knowledge thereof—but as the last link in a virtuous good, clean, and fair supply chain. What is this if not the building of a network, of a number of interconnected networks, the liberation of food from the free market?

One thing in particular struck me about networks, virtual and real, in the USA. It happened during my last trip, to Denver, Colorado. Matt Jones, a member of the local convivium and a new international board member, has long been a self-styled food activist. He has built up a local network, helping to bring Denver's many urban farming communities to Terra Madre. Visiting one of these one day, I immediately noted what a lot of people—mainly youngsters—were working in a field, all pulling up weeds. I was curious and asked one of them what he was doing there. "I'm a volunteer," he said. Matt told me the people were a "crop mob." I only have a smattering of English, and I was not particularly conversant with the concept of flash mobs, whereby a group of people, summoned via the Internet or by cell phone, suddenly assemble in a public place to stage some sort of happening together. A crop mob, Matt explained, is based on the same principle, but involves calling up volunteers to do farming work. It is a network of people who would like to work the land—farmers or former farmers, gardeners, or just people who want to find out more about their food—but have no land to work. When a job requiring a great deal of labor needs to be done—like weeding an organic field or picking fruit and vegetables—a crop mob is called in and dozens, sometimes hundreds, of people turn up to do it. They are provided with a meal, water, and drinks, plenty of music, and a chance to party once the day's labor is at an end.

The crop mob was invented in 2008 in a region of North Carolina known as the Triangle, the points of which are Raleigh, Durham, and Chapel Hill. I had been there in 2007 to present my book *Slow Food Nation*, and even then the Eat Local Triangle was a very active group of cooks, farmers, and activists. The From Fork to Table picnic that I took part in on that occasion was not only a mixture of farmers' market and *fête champêtre* (county fair) with all the customary games and raffles and a super US-style barbecue, but also an important celebration of the network that was coming into being and already boasted a number of members. One could see that something very important and new was being set in motion, combining the classic forms of the southern rural tradition with new technologies and media. I was amazed by the number of young people there.

It is no coincidence that crop mobs were born in the rural southern states of America as, basically, they replicate community practices that were also to be found in the Italian countryside years ago. Maybe the memory of these social conventions is fresher down South because farming society went into crisis later there. When hard work had to be done, the whole community would rally together, and workers who had just finished threshing or harvesting would go to help their neighbors without asking anything in return. The custom has disappeared as forms of industrial agriculture and intensive mechanization have gradually dispersed farming communities. But organic cultivation and the pursuit of sustainable processes require people, hence a community.

Organizing a crop mob in the urban farms of Denver holds an even deeper significance. It is mind-blowing to see young business executives spending their weekends tugging up weeds in a suburban field. Their work hides a desire to get back to the land and to food, to feel a part of something, of a community, which in the case in point often meets on the Internet too, communicating by Twitter and Facebook, but then comes together in the fields, in flesh and blood, in these special moments. It is the 2.0 version of what used to be the norm in the countryside before "modernization," in the days when it still had a human dimension. It still exists in many parts of the world, the "lesser developed," but seeing it reproduced in this form in a metropolis of the size of Denver shows that it is more than nostalgia that we are talking about. On the contrary, we are talking about *new* paradigms and ways of making food, of claiming back values that we thought had been lost.

Who knows if they will ever take off in Italy, these crop mobs? A free network sets no limits on creativity and is never afraid to look backward to go forward. One thing is for sure: the United States is an incredible laboratory for these experiences, which have already made the return journey to Europe to change ways of farming here. Luckily, the presence and influence, in these worlds and in these networks, of Terra Madre communities are contagious, spreading positive messages and the freedom to draw on diversity to make progress and innovate. But is this true innovation? Seeing the satisfied, happy faces of the crop mobbers in Denver at the end of the day as they danced to bluegrass and ate freshly picked vegetables cooked by the urban farmer's wife, I believe it is. It is a new happiness.

# CHAPTER 6

# A NIGHT AT SALONE DEL GUSTO–TERRA MADRE 2012

On Saturday, October 27, 2012, we were in the middle of the Salone del Gusto and Terra Madre. Living the event as president of Slow Food is at once exhilarating and exhausting. All the humanity of our network is there—hence an ever-multiplying number of opportunities for talking to people and exchanging views—but the vastness of the exhibition area obliges one to walk miles from one stand to another in an uninterrupted sequence of private appointments and public conferences, of meetings and Taste Workshops. One minor paradox is that for many people who work there the Salone—as the event is referred to confidentially in the Slow Food offices—is the least "food-related" moment of the year. They often have to skip lunch and sometimes they almost forget to eat at all, or simply do not have time to. These are the contradictions of a life that, at times, gets a little too fast for we who preach slowness. Not that it is a problem as, for us, the real nourishment comes from finding ourselves face to face with the world's food producers, with the Terra Madre communities, with the many members and convivium leaders, who have to be thanked wholeheartedly for the voluntary work they do in their local areas—and that they are all volunteers is a fact always worth remembering. The network is there before our very eyes, so it is no big deal if there is no time for anything else.

The only chances one has to sit back and relax are in the evenings after dinner, when all the scheduled official engagements are over and one can let oneself go. Then begin the rare, "casual" commitments that often prove more constructive than the formal ones. Often one indulges in idle chat, unconcerned about staying up late, even if the next day is going to be endless, completely dedicated to the event, and will start with an early wake-up call. After all, the Salone is held every two years and no opportunity can be missed.

Let me go back to that Saturday evening. I had spent the day dashing back and forth to and from all four corners of Lingotto Exhibition Center and the Oval, the space of about 80,000 square meters in Turin where we have always held this, our flagship event. On top of everything, that was also the first day of the last International Congress, which I have mentioned more than once previously, and a welcome dinner had been organized for the delegates from all over the world. Back in my hotel, also in the Lingotto area of Turin, my closest collaborators, who I always have around me on these occasions, and I sat down for the ritual last drink of the day, to sum up the day past and plan meetings for the day after. It often happens on these occasions that people on their way to bed—friends, exhibitors, collaborators, cooks, important guests—sacrifice an hour or so of sleep to stop for a little extra chat.

At a certain point on the night in question, the then Minister of Agricultural and Forestry policies, Mario Catania, was walking by. He had only been appointed a short time before, but he had long been a functionary at the Ministry and was sincerely happy to be at the Salone del Gusto and Terra Madre. Unlike many of his colleagues, who tend to have a "hit-and-run" approach to the inaugurations of major events, he had decided to stay on for an extra day to get a better idea. I mention this episode simply because it was on that night that I got a clear sense of how networks can work and the power they can wield from the grassroots upward.

After hearing his impressions on the Salone, I spoke with the minister about the so-called "land-saver" bill he had just tabled in parliament in the first attempt ever in Italy to issue a law aimed at curbing land consumption. His proposals had caused a big stir over the previous two days and a few gaps in his draft bill had incurred the wrath of Italian environmentalists. I do not wish to dwell here on the details of the bill—following the subsequent well-known political events and the consequent change in government,[23] it has since been left to gather dust in desk drawers at the ministry—except to say that the document has one historic feature. It cannot be said to have marked a victory, but at least it ruffled what seemed to be unrufflable. In an article in *La Repubblica* in December 2012, I rattled off a set of staggering figures about the land consumption in Italy. According to a report published by the Ministry of Agricultural and Forestry Policies, in fact, from 1971 to 2010 we had lost 28 percent of our agricultural land, an area as big as Lombardy, Liguria, and Emilia-Romagna put together, while every day 100 hectares of land were being built over:

---

[23] Mario Catania was a member of Prime Minister Mario Monti's government of technocrats, assembled in 2011 to address the Italian debt crisis. The government fell out of power following the General Election in March 2013 and was replaced by a coalition led by Enrico Letta.

What follows is intended as a cry of suffering against local area and agricultural land consumption in all its shapes and forms, the biggest environmental and cultural catastrophe a helpless Italy has witnessed for decades. For if agricultural land disappears, the ensuing disaster is nutritional, hydro-geological, environmental, and natural. It is like being indebted for life and indebting one's children and grandchildren to boot.

The problem dovetails with the general crisis that has been afflicting Italian agriculture for some years now, seeing how all its sectors are in trouble [ . . . ] Let us remember that when we defend agriculture, we are not defending a beautiful (or rough) old world of the past, we are defending our country, our chances of forming communities at the local level, and a future in which we can still hope to experience real well-being and witness great beauty.

This is why the moment has come to say enough is enough: I would like to propose a national moratorium against the consumption of free land and I sincerely hope it will be emanated [ . . . ] Strong action is needed, a petition or a firm declaration to stop forever the disappearance in our country of agricultural land, of ugly, useless building, of shopping centers that dehumanize us as men and women and turn us into solitary and debased automata-cum-consumers.

If we manage to get through the present appalling political situation unscathed, the moratorium should be made official by the Agriculture, the Environment, and the Cultural Heritage Ministries jointly, because our territory is the first cultural heritage of this, a Nation about to celebrate its 150th birthday. I am certain that the many organizations that are working in this direction, like my own, Slow Food, or, for example, the Stop al Consumo del Territorio (No to Land Consumption) network, the Italian Environmental Fund, environmental associations, farmer's associations, and the myriad civic committees scattered all over the country will agree and be prepared to join forces. The moment is ripe to launch a joint campaign to oversee the land extensively and at a local level to amplify the cry of millions of Italians sick and tired of seeing the land-scapes and places they love being destroyed, yet another of the forms of oppression we suffer, even for what is free and priceless—beauty. Look around you: beauty is every-where, especially in the small things before our very eyes. It is a form of poetry available everywhere that we should not allow ourselves to be deprived of, that deserves respect and devotion, that saves our souls every day.

That cry of suffering did not go unheeded. The network I was calling for to unite all the forces in Italy engaged in the defense of free land and the landscape was officially constituted in October 2011. In slightly less than a year, it became the Italian Forum for the land and landscape, spawning the ongoing "Let's save the landscape, let's defend local areas" campaign. Today more than 800 national and local Italian associations are involved in it. There are also more than 100 committees that steward local areas made up of people from the most diverse associations and bodies. The campaign's website, which con-stantly reports episodes of damage and destruction from the various provinces, not to mention about the mobilization underway, has become the most authoritative source for news on the subject. A challenging "Census against cement" cam-paign has been launched to make a precise update of the Italian property situation. There would appear to be 10 million houses standing vacant, even as construction work and speculation continue—though the crisis has slowed down the process. All Italian municipalities were asked to supply the data in their possession but, though more than a year has gone by, only a small percentage have responded. The campaign is going ahead nonetheless. Since the Forum was constituted, the intention has been to draw up a bill by popular initiative calling for a moratorium on the consumption of free land. Slowly but surely, the Forum is working on the project and accepts contributions from anybody prepared to make them. The effectiveness of its pressure and communication campaigns may be judged from the fact that one of minister Catania's first commitments was precisely the bill, which took the Forum by surprise and undoubtedly represented an overture to its urgent demands.

As I said, I have no intention here of discussing the merits of the bill but when, that night in Turin, Mario Catania pressed me to make my own contribution to the bill and correct its defects, virtually making me the spokesperson for the Forum and the criticisms and suggestions it was putting forward, that made me understand the strength of networks even more. As it soldiers along between ups and downs and a series of "sovereignty" issues that I shall return to later, the Forum nonetheless deserves credit for posing a central question that nobody was talking about, for the first time in history, putting it on the agenda of an Italian government. Many associations—some more, others less—have shelved their own specific claims to work together for a common goal, involving their grassroots at a local level and letting loose impressive communicational firepower at national level.

Before being mothballed after the fall of Mario Monti's government, the bill was extensively amended by the Italian State-Regions Conference, which, needless to say, implemented all the revisions proposed by the Forum—no mean feat. The battle continues to rage and all its effects have yet to be felt. With the advent of the new government, and despite the gloomy political climate, a large number of different bills on the subject have been lodged, supported by various parliamentary groups of different political colors. At least now we can say that the situation is no longer as stagnant as it was. Indifference has been overcome and land consumption is on the political agenda. Let us see what happens next.

Returning to that Saturday night at the Salone del Gusto-Terra Madre, ten seconds after I had said good night to the minister, by an odd coincidence who should turn up next but the European Commissioner for Agricultural and Rural Development, Dacian Cioloş, followed by an entourage of collaborators. He had delivered a speech at the inauguration of our conference that morning and, after visiting the Salone and dining at a top Turin restaurant, he was now going to his room. But after greeting me warmly, he was happy to sit down for a drink.

# CHAPTER 7

# THE CAP

After corresponding with Cioloş just after his election as European Commissioner, I had met him personally for the first time when he came to the Salone del Gusto-Terra Madre event in Turin in 2010. He had accepted the invitation immediately and, right from our first very informal exchange of civilities to his speech to the plenary meeting at the opening of Terra Madre, he impressed everyone present for the way his views were in tune with those of Slow Food. We all had great hopes that he would be able to drive the reform of the CAP, the Common Agricultural Policy, toward greater equity, justice, and sustainability, as everyone opposed to industrial and industrialist agricultural production had been hoping for years.

That night in Turin in 2012 it was precisely the CAP reform that we spoke about. The Commission had drawn up its first reform proposal and published it exactly a year earlier, in November 2011, and the debate was now heating up. We were halfway through the process that eventually was to lead, in June 2013, to the passing of an unsatisfactory, lame reform. If, on the one hand, it introduced elements of novelty and showed concern for ecology, for young people, and for the streamlining of bureaucratic red tape, on the other, it maintained the status quo. Meaning that the largest slice of the subsidy pie (more than 40 percent of the entire European Union budget) still ends up in the pockets of a few farmers, the largest land-owners and the champions of the most unsustainable agriculture possible. Though Cioloș did buck the trend slightly, equity and, as a consequence, sustainability were conspicuous by their absence. The question of care for the environment, one of the most important duties for farmers, who depend on nature for their work, did manage to force its way into the reform. Though it continues to be generally incomplete and unsatisfactory (to the extent that many decisive questions have been left to Member States to solve for themselves, almost as if the policy were not "common" after all), the reform does include so-called "greening" measures, which, albeit insufficient and weakened by subsequent revisions, insofar as they are bound to the direct subsidies that farmers should receive, do represent a first historical signal of concern for the question.

When I asked him that night how he thought things would pan out, Cioloș replied, "I know fine and well that there are forces moving in an entirely different direction, but if just one of the key points that we added at the Commission stage were to go through, for me it would be a great victory." He went on to give me an object lesson on what politics means at certain levels: namely the art of mediation and pursuit of a compromise as far as possible satisfactory. It was illuminating to listen to him, even though I was beginning to feel a sense of disillusionment. But this did not stop our commitment; in fact, this is what I wish to talk about now vis-à-vis the free network.

In 2010, looking ahead to the reform described above, Slow Food began to prepare what, in the halls of power in Brussels, they call a position paper, a long document listing the priorities we felt the CAP should address. These can be summed up as: small- and medium-scale agriculture; incentives for youth employment; protection of biodiversity; less free enterprise and new paradigms; a policy combining agriculture and food with a holistic approach; fewer injustices in the distribution of subsidies; total attention to "green" issues. The document was sent to all European members of parliament and all the members of the commissions involved. We received occasional responses and succeeded in sensitizing politicians to issues deemed to be of secondary importance, but actually decisive for the distribution of almost half the public money—our money included—available to the EU. "Public money for public goods" soon became one of our slogans and, in this case, when I say "our" I am not only referring to Slow Food and Terra Madre.

Since 2010, in fact, we have been part of the ARC2020 (Agricultural and Rural Convention 2020) platform, a network of more than 150 associations from 22 Member States of the European Union, which meet to put pressure on the European institutions and shore up CAP reform campaigns. The experience has been an important one since it has added a continental and international dimension to our demands, and our sharing of intents has been total. ARC2020 has never spoken on behalf of its single member associations, but has brought their voices together as one, performing the difficult task of monitoring complicated European procedures and bureaucratic jargon, putting pressure on European members of parliament through campaigns and positive lobbying activities, and supplying documentation to anyone keen to find out more about a subject that is difficult but also decisive for the destiny of European agriculture and food. It does so by involving citizens as much as possible, supplying them with information and urging them to play an active part. This was the case of "Go M.a.D.," a campaign to provide people with the wherewithal to contact their Euro members of parliament directly and ask them how they intended to vote on the reform and why.

With ARC2020 we organized public demonstrations such as the "Good Food March" through the streets of Brussels, a colorful procession of farmers who had come from all over Europe to assert their demands in front of EU headquarters. In more than one official meeting I have spoken on behalf of ARC2020 to members of the various commissions and to the *rapporteurs*, the people who actually wrote the reform. We have succeeded for the first time in making the voice of civil society heard loud and clear in the corridors of power, which have always been somewhat removed from reality and where they speak their own special brand of multilingual bureaucratese. For common citizens it is hard just to scratch the surface of this world, never mind penetrate it. The networking experience with ARC2020 has been one of the best we have had in recent years, and it gives me pleasure to speak about a network other than our own. Every association that joined the platform—there were environmentalists, organic and biodynamic farmers, and consumers—sacrificed a piece of its own sovereignty and specific aims to pursue an urgent and common objective.

There is still a lot of work to be done and the CAP reform hardly lived up to our expectations. Nonetheless, it is still possible to work on the implementation of regulations that have been left to single Member States to decide. In the meantime, we scored an important success in July 2013 when we took part in the last meeting of the High-level Steering Board of the European Innovation Partnership on Agricultural Productivity and Sustainability at the European Commission, in particular at the Directorate-General for Agriculture. On that occasion, six months of hard work resulted in the passing of the Strategic Implementation Plan for innovation, which will establish the criteria for allocating resources in research and innovation in agriculture under the CAP reform over the period 2014–2020. My sherpa—I do not like the term, but this is what technical assistants are called in the EU world—Michele Antonio Fino, a lecturer in Roman and Ancient Law representing the University of Gastronomic Sciences in Pollenzo and Slow Food, has worked hard with NGOs that are fellow members of ARC2020, all committed to defending biodiversity, soil fertility, traditional skills, and noncommercial agriculture. We managed to have the text that was about to be approved revised, introducing important elements for the protection of small farms that seek more than just profit. It was a very tough battle, but working as a network we managed to pull off a victory that was anything but a foregone conclusion and is sure to prove decisive for the distribution of sizable European resources over the next few years.

The European network that has grown up around the CAP reform is still as lively as ever. The experience has been a fruitful one, during which we have built up a set of contacts, competences, and relations, and together we have performed a monumental task. Not that we shall be stopping here; as the name of the platform says, our target is 2020.

On that one night, October 27, 2012, while outside the hotel the humanity of the two networks we have created, Salone del Gusto and Terra Madre, was going off to bed, I had had the chance to talk to two of the leading players in Italian and international agricultural policy thanks to the backing of the people I had behind me and close to me: the people of free networks that intersect, build knowledge and information, and are capable of mobilizing when necessary. On your own, even if there are a lot of you, you count for little. This is something that not everyone can get their head around, as often it involves either bearing a standard or planting it in a project. Some people see good ideas as if they were their offspring and find it hard to accept that, at a certain point, they have to start walking on their own two feet, to leave home and go off with others. If you are not prepared to accept that, you will never change the world. You have to be prepared to sacrifice something to create a larger whole.

# CHAPTER 8

# FREE, BUT FREE FOR REAL

I realize I may have seemed somewhat self-referential so far, and I hope the reader will excuse me. The fact is that I have simply spoken about what I have seen and experienced first-hand, about what, in my opinion, has changed the world of gastronomy, and the central role of food over the last three decades. I have done so from my own point of view, exploiting the privileged observation post Slow Food and Terra Madre give me. Read in a broader historical perspective, the facts I detail show how changes have multiplied at lightning pace over the last few years. With the passing of time and after every journey I make, discovering the people who combine to form the Slow Food–Terra Madre network is an experience I feel very fortunate to be living, an experience I wish to share with you.

Since our somewhat adventurous beginnings and our first escapades in the 1980s, the world has changed profoundly, as has our way of considering food. It is precisely thanks to the ways in which the world has evolved that what was unthinkable then for gastronomes like us, keen to assert the right to pleasure and claim a new dignity for the science they were upholding, has actually come to pass. Farmers from every continent have gathered together at Terra Madre, while inside the network new contacts and other energy flows—new swarms!—have emerged, drawing in associations of every type, informal groups, food and local communities real or virtual. Links with other portions of the world, with other networks, stray off into unexplored points, just like the roots of a tree, and ramify upward like the branches of a tree, bearing fruits unhoped-for and unimaginable twenty years ago.

Our network is playing a prominent role at many of the salient moments of our times, interfacing with the most innovative trends and grassroots movements. It is no coincidence that it is spreading, with no outside impetus, in many of the so-called BRIC and CIVETS countries, seen by economists as representative of two tiers of new development. Brazil, Russia, India, and China are the BRIC countries, ahead of Colombia, Indonesia, Vietnam, Egypt, Turkey, and South Africa, the CIVETS countries. I am certain that however hard we try, we shall never be able to grasp the magnitude of change in real time. Nonetheless, it is our mission to make the effort, and the networks help us to do this. So far I have told stories about Brazil, India, Indonesia, and Turkey, countries identified as being among the most rapidly developing in the world, but the network is present everywhere: in Europe, in North America, and even in countries deemed backward. I shall tell some of their stories in the next chapter.

What I am at pains to clarify is why I speak of a "free" network. I have already explained how Slow Food has been obliged, despite itself, to fuse with the communities of Terra Madre that it was helping to connect, and how this happened officially for the first time at the last International Congress. This was a strategic, obviously somewhat forced fusion, but I wish to stress that it was made neither to favor Slow Food and its growth nor to favor Terra Madre. In short, I am not afraid that the association that I preside over, which I founded, and which, insofar as it represents virtually my whole life, I am obviously very attached to, may one day dissolve into the "liquid" form of the free network: into Terra Madre and, above all, into all the networks and swarms that Terra Madre comes into contact with around the word. What the food communities do is not the merit of Slow Food; the merit belongs to the communities themselves, because they have always been doing it and it is their job to do it. This is why I like to talk of "austere anarchy": no one is in a position to teach anyone anything, even though there is a lot to be learned through reciprocal knowledge, democratic discussion, and exchanges of experiences.

If Slow Food does have a merit, it is that of connecting nodes, at least of trying to connect them. I would not be afraid one day of saying, "Slow Food is dead, long live Slow Food!" because that would mean that the project had grown so much as to be unmanageable by a single structure, that it had assumed a value and dimensions so global as to have spread and shared its practices everywhere. It would mean that it had been absorbed by the network, but without foregoing its values and its missions. Above all, I hope its "affective intelligence," which, after all, is an intelligent way of being brothers and sisters—of loving each other—never disappears. Believe me, it is possible to breathe and feel this sentiment at every single one of our gatherings, from the twice-yearly meetings in Turin to visits to the most out-of-the-way communities.

I am not afraid of liberating more diversity, and I am not afraid if "liberated gastronomy" progresses as a science and as an approach to life. I am not afraid because I am beginning to see real changes in the most unlikely places and at the most unlikely distances. I can also see a new perspective ahead—a perspective that was unforeseeable for us at the beginning and still unconceivable for many now—which will shape the history of this world. Good ideas travel far, and many, many people have good ideas at every latitude. The secret is to join forces. I am not afraid that the present organizational form of our network may still be inadequate, because Terra Madre has shown it can go a step further, and I have faith in it. I would not be afraid even if it had no organizational form anymore.

This free, liquid network is quite simply a phenomenal tool, a way offered to us by globalization to weave new relations and exchanges on equal terms, without anyone wishing to predominate and allowing us to set ourselves the highest targets. As early as 2005, I was speaking about the network in my book *Slow Food Nation* (pp. 205–206):

> Let us be clear about one thing: the plan is not to build a network to which we can then attach an ideological label (much less a trademark, new or existing), but to lay the foundations for a network perfectly able to increase in "intensity and extent," and in which expansion is guaranteed in proportion to the diversity that it is able to absorb.

> The democratic nature of the network is guaranteed by the equal status of all the subjects involved, who are all considered—because they consider themselves to be such—gastronomes in equal measure [ . . . ] the world network of gastronomes, as we call it, is at the same time local and global, diverse and united, concerned with details and the whole—with food at its center. It is virtuous, in other words it works for creation and not for destruction; it desires to increase the range of sharing and will not generate new divisions. It is a network that can link up with all the other virtuous networks [ . . . ].

No ideological label, no banner, still less the snail symbol—we cannot in any way regiment the energy we have helped release and liberate. All we can do is have faith in it. One reason for this is that, as history is demonstrating, this force invariably beats us on the field, leaving us to see how some seeds have borne good fruits, to work to channel energies more effectively so that today's main project, the only real objective our society can set itself, can be achieved. This is the new perspective a global movement of gastronomes has to aim at: we have to free ourselves of the slavery of hunger and malnutrition.

We gastronomes, as we define ourselves, cannot remain indifferent to a planetary injustice that cries out for revenge every day God sends us. All those who put food at the center of their lives because they regard it as indispensable not only for survival, but also as a key part of their values, identity, and culture, are obliged to make a contribution, however small it may be—like avoiding waste, for example. Fortunately, many communities that suffer this planetary scourge are hard at work to show us that they are capable of coming through on their own, with total sovereignty and territorial specificity. It is no coincidence that the means at their disposal, and the concepts they embrace, coincide with many of the specificities of our own liberated gastronomy. These ideas can be turned into the "gastronomy of liberation," an immediate future that is already reality in many places, the promise of long-term changes that we have to favor, feed, spread, guard, and oversee.

A network of 10,000 nodes is, above all, a symbol of our commitment for people inside Slow Food and Terra Madre. On May 15, 2013, the director general of the Food and Agriculture Organization (FAO), José Graziano da Silva, invited me to Rome to sign what, for us, was a historic official collaboration agreement with the organization. The document is a detailed protocol of the activities developed jointly over the next few years. It focuses largely on the creation of awareness campaigns, the bolstering of production and sales networks in struggling countries, the celebration of 2014 as the International Year of Family Agriculture, and, above all, participation in the "Zero Hunger Challenge" program. This is a challenge for us, too, and we intend to address it with the "gastronomy of liberation" behind us.

# IV. THE GASTRONOMY OF LIBERATION

## CHAPTER I

# ON LIBERATION

For me, the signing of the agreement between FAO and Slow Food on May 15, 2013, was a very important event indeed. In the annals of the movement I founded and preside over, the date marks a historic turning point. It was at once the point of arrival and departure of an awareness that has developed along the journey that we embarked upon with Terra Madre, the network in which we began to think about the role that "liberated gastronomy" might have, following the criteria of "good, clean, and fair," in fighting famine and malnutrition.

I am sure that many old-school gourmets or gastronomes will find jarring, to say the least, the idea that Slow Food can and must commit itself to this complex and ambitious civilizing mission. Yet our idea of gastronomy cannot ignore the universal right of people to eat adequately and according to their cultures. It is a worldwide problem and the inability to solve it is a total scandal that cannot leave a true gastronome indifferent. Luckily, we are receiving more and more encouragement from bodies such as FAO and IFAD, the International Fund for Agricultural Development, the United Nations agency that funds rural development projects. Both have called on us over the last few years to give life to fruitful, profitable collaborations.

Their choice is indicative of a conviction that is growing among major international institutions that the agricultural policies implemented in the past in the so-called "developing countries" now need to be drastically reviewed. After an encouraging beginning in the 1960s and 1970s, when they effectively improved the living conditions of farmers in some areas of the world, in the new millennium the pursuit of the paradigms of the Green Revolution and intensive production—firmly based on genetically selected vegetable varieties, widespread use of plant protection products and fertilizers, massive water consumption, and hefty investment in infrastructure—has betrayed all its ecological, economic, and social limits. The extensive use of chemicals and standardized products with a view to industrializing agriculture has not achieved the improvements hoped for. Over recent decades, hunger and malnutrition have continued to be rife, and new grave, unforeseen problems have emerged.

Even institutions such as FAO and IFAD are now convinced of the importance of revaluing the small-scale production of native vegetable varieties and livestock breeds, of family agriculture, of the role of women, of traditional practices, of subsistence economies. With relatively little effort and by virtue of all the diversity they represent, all these factors are keeping communities alive, both literally and metaphorically, in the world's most fragile, delicate contexts. My sensation that something is changing profoundly in the corridors of institutional power can be summed up by the fact that if, under the previous director general Jacques Diouf, all our invitations to FAO to take part in Terra Madre and enter into collaboration and dialogue fell on deaf ears, now certain international bodies are not only pleased to meet the food communities of our network and are prepared to learn from our way of practicing agriculture, but have often come to search us out. Before signing our agreement, the present director general of FAO, José Graziano da Silva, was keen to visit Pollenzo and, when he came, he delivered a *lectio* to the students of the University of Gastronomic Sciences in which he stressed that the political, economic, and technical paradigm for fighting world hunger and malnutrition is changing at last.

As I explained above, through its contacts with the communities of the Terra Madre network, Slow Food is a leading player in this far-reaching change. We have been in a privileged position to observe the advocates of this new beginning, and we realized what was happening immediately, or almost. The most interesting and also the most disruptive thing we noted was that, through a parallel process of reciprocal influence, our "liberated gastronomy" had become a tool of liberation: of liberation from poverty, from the free market, from colonial- and post-colonial cultural conditionings, from the impositions, restrictions, and serious defects of the global food system. In some cases, one is also beginning to glimpse a concrete liberation from hunger and malnutrition. This corroborates to no small degree the idea and the intent of placing gastronomy at the center of a battle of this scale, of gambling everything on gastronomy (what a great example of "unpairing of the cards"!) on a table that will decide the future of food and of billions of people.

Oddly enough—though, come to think of it, it may not actually be all that odd—the most celebrated elements of the manual of the classic gourmet (taste, appearance, fine culinary and productive processes), from which, somehow and for some time, we had to free ourselves to discover all the economic, social, ecological, and ethical implications of the food universe, are not an obstacle at all in certain contexts. On the contrary, they are proving useful for the redemption of traditional food cultures, until recently either regarded as inferior or completely ignored. An important tool of liberation for certain societies and local areas, even the most unlikely, is the exclusively gastronomic revaluation or rediscovery of biodiversity and local culinary traditions, according to formulas that have nothing to envy the world's finest restaurants.

The West may have witnessed something of this interplay between "high" and "low" gastronomy in times of which our only memory is in books of gastronomic history. It is a sort of melting pot of cultures, a birth of new identities in which exchange takes place at last on an equal footing, and the leading actors are fully conscious of the process underway, with all its social, economic, and ecological implications. It is a dialogue between North and South, between rich and poor, between tradition and new practices, between arcane, ancient, and ultramodern technologies, between various elements of gastronomic and rural culture, once forgotten but now retrieved and communicated in a new way. It is a very complex, constantly evolving dialogue that is leading to the redefinition of categories—though, eventually, we ought to abandon categories altogether—and, above all, changing the life of people and modifying the perspective of true gastronomes, who no longer confine themselves to tasting, but now use their senses as a powerful tool for interpreting the reality of the world.

In 2008, the Slow Food Foundation for Biodiversity produced a series of booklets of traditional African recipes for the communities and their countries of origin. The first was dedicated to argan oil in Morocco, the second to the culinary traditions of Mali. Today the project is sponsored by FAO and has developed into the "From Earth to Table" library, a series of four recipe books dedicated respectively to Mali, Sierra Leone, Guinea Bissau, and Senegal, all downloadable online. This is a simple but original way that no one had ever thought of before of reviving and disseminating across communities traditions that risked disappearing, and the use in the kitchen of the local agricultural products that inspired them, products supplanted by the foods and condiments of the multinational food industry. Like the stock cube, for example, which in the space of a couple of generations managed to erase the memory of many typical dishes that had hitherto ensured healthy and varied eating.

The success of these booklets during Terra Madre meetings and in the food communities themselves is very encouraging and helps support my case. What I wish to stress most here is how the practice of taking recipes, conceived structurally and textually in the style of classic gastronomy, to poor economies is an act of the highest dignity and, above all, sets into motion new mechanisms that promise great things for the future. For the first time ever, the humble domestic labor of African women is being documented and represented, and nothing prevents Africa's previously "weak" cuisines from competing locally—thereby redeeming communities—against the invasion of "strong" and "industrialized" Western cuisines which, albeit out of context, undermine and irremediably destroy traditional skills in a variety of ways. If we continue to use these dominant cuisines as our term of comparison, there will be no future for the poorest countries. If it is true, on the other hand, that, insofar as they express a sense of the land and agriculture and culture of communities, all the world's cuisines are entitled to equal gastronomic attention and sensitivity, then everything classic gastronomy has done for France and Europe from the time of Brillat-Savarin onward should now be done for Africa and Latin America, too.

In the Americas, from Mexico southward, this idea has budded and is ripening at an unbelievable speed. At first, I felt a certain sense of amazement when I saw for myself what was happening in virtually every country there at every level, thanks to the work of a "high" range of expensive, important restaurants and a "low" one of popular, peasant gastronomy, in both of which traditional agriculture is at the fore. These two "souls," the high and the low, are not divided; on the contrary, they collaborate and support each other through an alliance between restaurateurs and farmers whose tangible social impact is arguably without parallel anywhere else in the world.

Though these countries boast a long history of gastronomy, until a short time ago there was an element almost of censorship toward local gastronomic traditions. This was due at first to the influence of Spanish and Portuguese "colonizers," sharply characterized by the French model (which, for a long time, was also seen as the "international" model), then by a plethora of small, more pacific "invasions." To quote one astounding statistic, at the turn of the twentieth century, as many as 24 million Italians arrived in South America, and in many respects this alone caused a sort of food revolution. The South America Indian and native cuisines were superimposed by those of the first true invaders from the Iberian peninsula, by those of the descendants of Africans, then in some areas by those of Italians, Germans, Japanese, and so on, in a melting pot that has given rise to a unique and highly complex gastronomic syncretism, a world away from the linearity—especially from a historical point of view—of European traditions, the dominant French one first and foremost.

Today many good local cooks and chefs have plenty of international experience under their belts. They are growing aware of the complexity of their lands of origin, especially of their agriculture and primary ingredients, and are seeking to exploit their multiform roots to generate a style at once novel and grounded in tradition, tied to the countryside and the people who live there. The praise some of these cooks and chefs are now winning from food and wine critics around the world is on a par with that heaped upon recent culinary greats, from the chefs behind nouvelle cuisine to Ferran Adrià at his elBulli restaurant in Spain and René Redzepi, leader of the Nordic school. Critics are perfectly capable of appreciating their culinary genius, less so of appreciating the magnitude of what lies behind it. Nor do they realize that, if we wish to make hunger and malnutrition disappear from the face of the earth, it is wrong to turn one's nose up precisely at what lies in the background. In reality the work of these new cooks and chefs, already stars in their own right, hides a perfect prototype of what I like to call "gastronomy for liberation." It already exists in Peru, Mexico, Brazil, Colombia, Argentina, Venezuela, Ecuador, and Bolivia, and hopefully it will conquer the whole world—for as our story shows, it can apply *to the whole world*—alleviating the dramatic plight of the poorest masses. I realized all this eating at the restaurants of these cooks and chefs and, even more so, through my knowledge of the communities where they source their ingredients and with which they collaborate—thereby demonstrating a great sense of social responsibility.

# CHAPTER 2
# PARADIGMATIC PERU

**W**hen, during a tour of South America in 2011, some of the Terra Madre communities and Slow Food members told me they intended to meet up at Mistura, the International Gastronomic Fair in Lima, I decided to find out more about the event. Over the years, many of the Peruvian communities had taken part first in the Salone del Gusto, then in Terra Madre in Turin, but I had never associated them with Mistura.

This gastronomic fair is famous, above all, for being regularly attended by the big names in international haute cuisine. Ferran Adrià was one of the first to go there to launch the new Latin American food trend, which is featuring more and more in the specialized media. Today Mistura is the place to be, with hordes of journalists from every continent swarming there in a curious mass migration. But this incredible success is starting to betray not a few contradictions; sponsors, for example, include multinationals that are, to say the least, "suspect," while the organizers pay little heed to the environmental sustainability of the event as such. Though Mistura is beginning to attract criticism, especially from hardliners, it still stands out as an exception, not only for Peru, but also for South America and the world. When I attended, I discovered that it is an event where farmers, producers, livestock breeders, fishermen, and artisans gather to speak about the future of gastronomy and agriculture and food. The similarities with our own Terra Madre were immediately clear to me, and I was curious to learn more about the story behind the phenomenon. It was and is not easy to fully comprehend the extent and importance of the gradual progress made by a country, Peru, that is enjoying considerable expansion, but is still, in part—especially in some rural areas—bogged down by problems of malnutrition and food insecurity.

In 2007, APEGA, Sociedad Peruana de Gastronomía, was born. Its statute sets out the following aims:

> The Sociedad Peruana de Gastronomía has the purpose of bringing together the leading players in national gastronomy to promote sustainable development, inclusion, and our cultural identity through Peruvian cooking. Its aims are:
>
> - to promote Peruvian cooking as a basis of cultural identity and a factor of economic development, progress, and well-being for all Peruvians;
> - to promote the excellence of ingredients and safeguard our country's biodiversity;
> - to promote agro-pastoral gastronomic supply chains;
> - to help train the new generations of professionals committed to furthering our vision and values;
> - restore value to the small producer's role in the gastronomic supply chain and to the gastronomic contribution of regional cooking and street food.

I am convinced that these principles are paradigmatic of what liberated gastronomy can give life to in the four corners of the planet and thus become a tool of liberation. APEGA's is the manifesto of an association, of a group of gastronomes (cooks and chefs, university lecturers, enthusiasts, journalists) who are addressing the challenges the food system is posing to all the world's cuisines.

Not that APEGA finds itself alone in a gastronomic and political desert. On the contrary, it epitomizes a general sensitivity that has grown notably over the last 15 years, thanks to the work and charisma of a man who has to be recognized as the star player of the Peruvian food boom. His name is Gastón Acurio.

Gastón and his wife, Astrid, are the chefs at their Astrid y Gastón restaurant in Lima, and he is famous the world over as an initiator of what has been defined as "New Andean cuisine." The concept underlying Acurio's philosophy is as simple as it is revolutionary: in Peru, one of the world's most incredibly biodiverse countries, haute cuisine was still being identified with French, Italian, and even—given the influence of immigration from Japan to this part of South America—Japanese dishes.

Aside from ceviche, the famous national raw fish dish, all gastronomic references seemed to point to the Old Continent. This is what sparked the total change in paradigm, with Acurio making the bold decision to center his idea of cooking around Peruvian produce and the dishes of the local Indian-colonial mestizo gastronomic tradition. He thus began to include in his menu the fruits of the Amazon, the vegetables of the Sierra, and traditional indigenous recipes, all impeccably cooked and presented. He also established a rapport with small producers and began to support them directly. It was thus that Peruvian gastronomy began to set itself free, to break out of the "cage" of gastronomies wrongly considered as minor or bereft of history, to recover its role as a creator of identity and social redemption.

Acurio was arguably the first person in Peru to realize the huge importance of cooks and chefs and their central role in the world food system, and now he is backed by a whole band of younger colleagues. Just think that, according to the "World's 50 Best Restaurants" league table (also sponsored by a multinational), seven of the top fifteen chefs in Latin America are working in Lima. True, Astrid y Gastón is not accessible to the majority of the population and serves food at distinctly "Western" prices. Yet what may appear to be a contradiction fades away if we consider how Acurio's work is intimately connected with the fields and the humanity who work them, and how its ends are also educational. This set of factors transcends the simple experience of dining at Astrid and Gastón's restaurant, which is bowling over the world's food critics and whose food I, too, have had the great fortune of enjoying. Acurio represents the cutting edge of a solid, well-knit Peruvian network with extremely clear objectives that are shared by all, from the superchef to the humblest peasant.

True, the unanimous, immediate consensus that almost all these cooks and chefs are receiving risks breaking the bank; dangers of perverting the sincere initial force of the phenomenon are always lying in ambush, and its leading players will have to ask themselves what road they intend to take in the years ahead to avoid "burning out" or, indeed, "selling out." For the moment, however, its impact has been undeniably revolutionary.

Valorizing the work of small Peruvian farmers who continue to grow native ancestral species means making them important figures in the definition of a national identity, and restoring them to their role as stewards of techniques, seeds, and knowledge that have been handed down through the centuries and constitute the backbone of national culture. New Andean cuisine is a culinary style with marvelous recipes and dishes, but it is also, and above all, a form of liberation from the dictates of European classic gastronomy, often incapable of grasping the political importance of food, of how it is produced and processed.

It was these reflections that spurred APEGA to act, and it was in their wake that Mistura came into being. But the story does not end here—far from it. It is no coincidence that the "Open letter to the cooks of tomorrow," the so-called Declaration of Lima cited at the end of the first chapter, should be signed in the Peruvian capital. Nor is it a coincidence that Lima is a candidate—another of APEGA's objectives—to become the gastronomic capital of Latin America in 2021, the bicentennial of Peruvian independence.

Here I wish to take the reflection further. Speaking about local food products and small farmers in Peru is not the same as speaking about them in Italy, because the two realities are separated by three centuries of colonization. Conquistadores of every provenance always considered local religion, eating habits, and social customs as things to be eliminated, as throwbacks to a backward, ignorant world, inferior and negligible from the ethnocentric point of view they brought from the Old World. This is why the revaluation of local gastronomy is so important. We are not speaking here of an exercise in chauvinism or nationalism designed to develop pride in identity, as sterile as it would be pointless. In the last few years Peru has made an extraordinary journey of awareness and redemption: of awareness because the connection between food and environment, social justice, and economic sustainability has emerged loud and clear; of redemption because putting local cooking at the center again has created economic prospects for a large section of the population hitherto relegated to conditions of extreme poverty.

It is comforting to note that in the wake of these crossovers, politicians, too, are now beginning to realize how vital it is to liberate gastronomy. In some rural regions, malnutrition is still a real problem, even though on June 16, 2013, the director general of FAO, José Graziano da Silva, awarded Peru, together with Armenia, Azerbaijan, Cuba, Djibouti, Georgia, Ghana, Guyana, Kuwait, Kyrgyzstan, Nicaragua, Saint Vincent and Grenadines,

Samoa, Sâo Tomé and Príncipe, Thailand, Turkmenistan, Venezuela, and Vietnam with a certificate for achieving in advance both the First Millenium Development Objective of cutting the number of people suffering from hunger by half by 2015 and the one established by the World Food Summit of cutting the total number of undernourished people by 2015.

According to the *State of Food Insecurity in the World 2014* report, published jointly by the UN's three Rome-based agencies—FAO, IFAD, and WFP (World Food Program)—805 million people around the world were still suffering from malnutrition and hunger: though it had fallen slightly, it was nonetheless a staggering figure. Great steps forward had been made in Latin America and the Caribbean, with the number of the undernourished dropping from 68.4 million in 1990–92 to 37 million in 2012–14, from 15.3 percent of the population to 6.1 percent. But, at the same time, the report showed that, at a global level, the rate of advancement toward the First Millennium Objective had slowed down. In Peru the situation had improved rapidly, but according to the report, 8.7 percent of the population was still undernourished (against 31.6 percent in the two-year period from 1990–92). This part of the population, as I said, lives mostly in rural areas, where difficult environmental conditions further sully the picture.

The figures emerging from the FAO-IFAD-WFP report need to be interpreted with care, however, as they clearly show that most of the difficulties involved in accessing food originate from oscillations in food prices, which, needless to say, go hand in hand with the price of oil. What does this mean? It means that, if communities are deprived of their food sovereignty by the imposition of monocultures and commercial hybrids for exchange on the global free market, the communities themselves are made hostage to price swings, hence to speculation. It is no coincidence that, in their joint report, the three principal international agencies concerned with food and the fight against hunger specify that, to reduce hunger sustainably, it will be necessary for general economic growth to be accompanied by implementation of the agricultural sector.

Which is fine, but what kind of growth are we talking about exactly? The 2012 document at last stresses the value and importance of subsistence agriculture in promoting food sovereignty and, albeit tardily, is the first institutional document to acknowledge that "agricultural growth involving smallholders, especially women, will be most effective in reducing extreme poverty and hunger when it increases returns to labor and generates employment for the poor." Smallholders and women are put at the center because they are the stewards of techniques and knowledge adapted over the centuries to their local areas to feed their communities. This may appear a minor point, but the fact that leading international agencies are prepared to acknowledge this aspect in an official document signifies that our network's almost thirty years' work is beginning to yield fruits.

In 2013, the Peruvian government launched "Quali Warma," a Ministry of Development and Social Inclusion program to improve school meals. On the premise that school meals are the main daily source of calories for many children, it had decided to revolutionize the way in which the system was organized. First in a few pilot schools, then nationwide, the food served in school cafeterias will henceforth come, as far as possible, from local suppliers, and the dishes prepared must belong to the culinary traditions of the single communities. This is a correct response to a school meal system hitherto dominated by industrial food products, mostly imported from abroad and produced by large multinationals capable of supplying all the school cafeterias in the country with a single tender, and at the same time of stuffing children with refined sugars and chemical additives, so-called *comida chatarra*, or junk food.

Professional chefs and the women and men of the communities have been called on to implement the project, elaborating a series of recipes suitable for the purpose in single districts and raising the profile of local agricultural produce as much as possible. Another linchpin of the project will be the planting of a garden in every school. Students will help cultivate and care for the plants, and the gardens will become a source of primary ingredients for the school canteens.

In April 2013, I was invited by the minister of Development and Social Inclusion, Carolina Trivelli, to Ayacucho to visit one of the first six schools in which the project was launched. I was accompanied by Sabrina Chavez, who had just been made a member of the Slow Food International Council. It was fantastic to see once more how pride, identity, joy, and passion can intertwine around liberated gastronomy. It was a revelation to taste dishes prepared by mothers, while their children explained to us how a certain tuber only grew in given inaccessible areas, or showed us how to make an otherwise bitter root edible. Restoring value to a community is, above all, a series of opportunities for restoring value to the way in which that community has nourished itself, preparing and consuming food, for centuries.

And thus, even as liberated gastronomy becomes the gastronomy of liberation, a tool of emancipation and valorization for local areas and communities, we have come the full circle—and not only in Peru.

# CHAPTER 3
# BACK TO BRAZIL

It is not only Mistura in Lima that is monopolizing international attention for the new wave of Latin American chefs and cooks who, as I have already mentioned, are scattered all over the continent. It is impossible, for example, not to speak about Brazil, a country that, under Lula's two administrations and with the present director general of FAO José Graziano da Silva presiding over the ministry dedicated to the Fome Zero (Zero Hunger) project, managed to eliminate malnutrition (and hunger) in the space of just a few years. On the gastronomic front, I enjoyed a wonderful experience in São Paulo from September 5–9, 2012, during the ninth annual Semana Mesa SP, a series of events organized by the food and wine magazine *Prazeres da Mesa*. The Semana is becoming an increasingly important opportunity for *nouvelle vague* chefs and cooks to meet and reflect, hence another catalyst of the lively new world of top-flight Latin American gastronomy.

I was accompanied by the new Slow Food International Council member Georges Schnyder, who works for the magazine and on a number of gastronomic and communication projects. He was my guide throughout days I will never forget. The topic of the week I took part in was *"Descobrindo as Américas; seus ingredientes e sua cultura"* (Discovering the Americas: Their Ingredients and Culture), which, on one hand, attracted special guests in the persons of top North American chefs (in previous years usually only Europeans had been invited), while on the other, focusing on work on the use and valorization of agricultural and wild food products closely bound up with local areas and the humanity that inhabits them. Slow Food was present in numbers in São Paulo. I personally delivered a speech on the question of networking and what it means to be in tune with the values of our international network of food communities, then the movement's vice-president, Alice Waters, spoke. In a talk much appreciated by the audience, she placed the emphasis on the founding principles of Slow Food, in particular on education through her Edible Schoolyards and the importance of clean proximity agriculture. Almost seven hundred people filled the conference hall every day, while the outside spaces were animated by exhibitions and small markets.

The chefs and cooks present were unanimous in their agreement on the topics discussed. If the North American guests were very much in line with Alice Waters, to all intents and purposes their guiding light, the Latin Americans were, if anything, even stronger, more political and propositional, in their views. First and foremost among them was, naturally enough, Gastón Acurio. His newfound awareness had evidently gotten even the great chef working with school gardens, thereby displaying a social commitment that, far from being cosmetic, was entirely functional to his project. This is just one of the signals that the new approach to food is starting to emerge from places inaccessible to the majority of the population to devise new, by no means "poorer" and less interesting, forms of popular catering. Rodrigo Oliveira and Wanderson Medeiros, two young chefs who are currently leading players on the Brazilian cooking scene, run cheap restaurants and, in their speeches at Semana Mesa SP, they expressed all the pride they feel at being pioneers, at taking elements of a new identity to the people by transcending the gastronomic styles imported from or imposed by the Old Continent.

For the occasion, even Alex Atala, a beacon in the new wave of Latin American cooking—though from the height of his renowned D.O.M restaurant he moves in very different directions—spoke about his collaboration with livestock breeders and farmers, praising local primary ingredients and explaining why they are so important. Argentines, Chileans, and Mexicans sang from the same songsheet. In this area of the world, we are witnessing an evolution that is marching parallel with the ideas of Slow Food and, thanks to Slow Food, also has a markedly social connotation. In São Paulo, for example, the Florianopolis convivium and the Slow Food Youth Network presented their work on connecting producers, cooks, and the young people of the favelas to turn gastronomy into something that adds zest to life and improves the prospects of people living in the less-well-off parts of the city. It is precisely in the favelas that the least elitist, most effective side of the new movement emerges.

At the end of the Semana Mesa SP conference, almost all the speakers moved on to Rio de Janeiro, to a large agglomerate of thirteen favelas known as Alemão, where 200,000 people live. The purpose of their trip was to inaugurate a new kitchen at the service of the community.

With the support of great Rio chefs—first and foremost, Kátia Barbosa of the Aconchego Carioca (a traditional *botequim* where the food is exceptional), and Claude Troisgros, brother of the multistarred French chef Michel, who moved here twenty years ago to open a hugely successful restaurant—the project will deliver quality catering for local parties. During the afternoon we spent at Alemão, we enjoyed an unforgettable party, animated by the cook Daniel Humm from New York, and Roberta Sudbrack, another star in the Brazilian culinary firmament. The convenient new cableway that is revolutionizing transport in Rio allowed us to avoid the warren of alleys that climb up among the humble abodes of these neighborhoods, and took us to the top of the hill that dominates part of the city. There in the sparkling new kitchens built for the project, our group was able to see at close quarters how it is possible to involve young people in the study of gastronomy and cooking, and thereby give them better-than-decent jobs and, maybe, to discover the talents of the future.

The project underway at Alemão reminded me of the one I had been so impressed by at Terra Madre Brazil 2010 in Brasilia. Five hundred delegates attended the event, where the star was David Hertz, a cook we have come to identify with Slow Food and Terra Madre (in which he took part for the first time in Turin in 2008). After traveling the world for years, living in a kibbutz in Israel and visiting China, Vietnam, India, Britain, and Canada, David returned to São Paulo and founded Gastromotiva, a "social business" that supplies catering and training services and sells community food products. It also provides youngsters in need or with problems at home an opportunity to study, find jobs, or even set up businesses. All profits are reinvested either in the training school or to open charity shops, and hence improve the food supply in the degraded favelas. In 2004, David presented a project at the Anhembi Morumbi University, one of the most important in Brazil, for the opening of a kitchen in the Jaguaré favela. He went on to raise funds from private citizens and non-profit organizations and has now established his cooking school as a full-fledged business whose guidelines are social inclusion, education, and training. The Gastromotiva bufé, or catering service, closes the sustainability circle by sourcing food products from local producers and family companies that practice agro-ecology. Yes, Brazil's new gastronomic entrepreneurs really do come from the favelas.

Anyone outside his country of origin who swoons over the cooking of Alex Atala, Roberta Sudbrack, Virgilio Martínez (another up-and-coming Peruvian who took part in Salone del Gusto–Terra Madre in 2012), Gastón Acurio, Enrique Olvera (in Mexico), and all the many others who are conquering the world stage—though, don't get me wrong, all the praise they receive is well deserved—is often unaware of the fact that the cultural movement they are part of and of which they are the most spectacular exponents has espoused all the precepts of "liberated gastronomy," implementing them to achieve new, continuous liberations. The connection with small producers, the defense of native biodiversity, work on tradition and identity as a fruit of continuous exchange, projects of social commitment—these are just some of the ingredients that make the birth of the gastronomy of Latin American liberation so revolutionary.

The results on the plate are amazing and are often a positive surprise for the gourmet's palate. Made with the produce of Brazil's Mata Atlantica, the Argentine *pampas*, the Peruvian Andes, the Chilean *cordigliera*, and Amazonia, the cooking offers novel tastes and sensations. It is the pride and joy of a heritage that, for us and for many Latin American city dwellers, is still largely unexplored, but is now coming to the fore with determination and creativity. Yet we are only at the beginning: it is now necessary to eschew all forms of superciliousness and follow the movement with great attention. In short, we have to decolonize our imaginations, exactly as its protagonists have done.

# CHAPTER 4

# IN MEXICO

During my visit to Mexico in 2013, I was invited to Morelia en Boca, a gastronomic event that takes place every year in Morelia, a city with a population of 800,000 inhabitants right in the center of the country. On my arrival I was welcomed with great pomp by the governor of the state of Michoacán, who subsequently took me around the fair. After a quarter of an hour of peregrinations among spic-and-span stands, winetasting rooms, a kitchen-cum-stage for demonstrations by great chefs, and makeshift restaurants, I was beginning to show a certain restlessness. I had the sensation that I was in the middle of one of those events, typical of the old "imprisoned" gastronomy, that have still failed to grasp the complexity of gastronomic sciences. It was still tied to an idea of pleasure unsustained by conscious responsibility. At the end of our reconnaissance tour of the Palacio Clavijero, the event venue, we ended up in a wing dedicated to the *cocineras de Michoacán*, the female cooks who keep watch over the Mexican gastronomic tradition.

In front of me were women cooking on an ancient wood-burning stove reminiscent of what in Piedmont we call a *putagé*, one of the greatest design objects in history (the only difference being that the one the women were using did not have a flue). They would cook all day breathing in the smoke from the fire, ruining their eyes and their lungs for the sake of visitors. Recognized by UNESCO as an Intangible Cultural Heritage of Humanity in 2010, Mexican gastronomy lays its roots and its virtues in the skills and know-how of women like these, in their manual dexterity and their knowledge. It is they who are the real heritage of humanity. Seeing the thankless task they were engaged in in Morelia aroused conflicting thoughts in me and in the collaborators who were with me.

On one hand, the recognition received in 2010 marked a step forward of extraordinary importance; the major international organization in the field had officially and definitively acknowledged that this astonishing mix of pre-Hispanic food preparations and culinary styles and traditions brought by the conquistadores is unique and inimitable and characteristic of this part of the world alone. On the other, it has triggered a series of mainly marketing operations that have turned the protagonists of this world, the cocineras tradicionales, into an attraction for tourists and visitors of fairs as opposed to something to be protected and appreciated. Proof of the fact is the often unhealthy environments in which they are forced to work.

Liberating gastronomy also means running this kind of risk, and no country or culture is immune from it. Suffice it to think of the media limelight conquered by food all over the world and the rash of TV programs that talk about it with disarming shallowness.

The recognition of Mexican gastronomy as a heritage of humanity begs another question that has to do with more than just Mexico. The Mexican diet is based on a few staple ingredients, among which the most representative of the national identity is undoubtedly maize (corn). Born in Mexico, maize subsequently spread all around the world thanks to its adaptability and versatility. These qualities did not escape the very first Spanish settlers in the country, who immediately took the new plant back to Europe. Yet if maize has arguably been the most successful plant in the world in terms of diffusion and use (today it is hard to find commercial food products that do not contain its by-products), its country of origin is now witnessing a startling contradiction.

Mexico, which currently imports 34.2 percent of its cereals (source: SOFI 2012), was self-sufficient for the production of maize until the entry into force of NAFTA, the North American Free Trade Agreement, in 1994. Though production has not decreased significantly, imports have increased exponentially from the United States, which until 2006 imposed dumping prices, 20 percent lower than production costs, to clear its subsidized surpluses. There has thus been an effective increase in both the production and the import of maize, which is now earmarked largely for animal feed and the food industry, not to mention the production of biofuel, and no longer ensures self-sufficiency for human consumption. The rigged prices at which U.S. maize was sold in Mexico until 2006 underwent a drastic upswing in 2007, following an increase in the price of maize in the United States due, in turn, to a rise in the international price of grain.

In Mexico, all this triggered an immediate rise in the cost of tortillas, a staple food in the diet of the Mexican poor, provoking a wave of protest, especially among the urban population. According to an inquiry ordered by the government to investigate speculation on the price of maize, multinationals such as Cargill and Bimbo had gone so far as to keep maize "hidden" in storehouses scattered around the country, ready to sell off when the price peaked on the world market. The government's only response was a sort of call to arms to increase the production of yellow maize, the world's best-known variety, but without having the decency to explain that yellow maize is used essentially for animal feed and biofuels. The nonstop price rises hit the poorest Mexicans hard in the pocket, obliging them to spend an increasing amount of their wages on food. This drove an increasingly large section of the population to rethink their eating habits and buy imported commercial food products (some made with transgenic soybeans and the by-products of maize), instead of traditional primary ingredients that had grown too expensive.

The damage to their health was enormous. Even as 2 million Mexicans were suffering from malnutrition (source: SOFI), the country was also recording an alarming increase in obesity among adults and children. Last year, an event occurred that was as historic as it was sad, with the obesity rate in Mexico reaching 32.8 percent, more than in the United States. According to FAO data, seven out of ten Mexican children are obese—yet another figure that can be attributed to the iniquity of the food system.

Luckily, the backlash of civil society has been far stronger than the response from the institutions. One offshoot is "*Sin maiz no hay país*," a network of Mexican associations coordinated by a number of NGOs, among which is Greenpeace, whose aim is to protect native maize species from the invasion of commercial hybrids. Slow Food is part of this network and has brought with it the blue corn producers of Ozolco, a cooperative that cultivates and processes blue maize (an Ark of Taste product) to sell both on the domestic market at Puebla and at the Slow Food Philadelphia convivium in the USA, with which it is twinned in the project. The network is fighting to hold back the excessive power of agro-industry in Mexico and, though the road ahead is still long and strewn with difficulties, alliances are being forged that promise great things for the future. The Coletivo Mexicano de Cocina, a group that brings together the most influential chefs in the country—Enrique Olvera and Jorge Vallejo, first and foremost—has also embraced the cause of the protection of native maize, using it and promoting it in their kitchens in the prestigious restaurants that feature in the new wave of Latin American cooking.

Many other projects are underway to defend and distribute traditional maize varieties, so that the question is now in the public domain and interest high, at last. Mesamerica, another major event entirely dedicated to cookery and gastronomy in a very broad sense, is devoting an increasing amount of space to aspects of the protection of small-scale farm produce and ancestral techniques such as *la milpa*, an integrated system for cultivating different plants sown in the same field so that each nourishes the other and, even in the event of disease to one or more varieties, the farmer is still left with plenty to eat. As Olvera, one of the world's top chefs who works at the Puyol restaurant in Mexico City, declared to Simone Bobbio of *Slow* magazine in an interview at the last Salone del Gusto and Terra Madre event:

> Agricultural production in Central America still uses the traditional milpa method, whereby maize, beans, pumpkins, tomatoes, and peppers grow simultaneously on the same plot of land. It is a system that requires no fertilizers or pesticides since the different species counterbalance one another, supplying and receiving nutritional substances, nitrogen in particular, simply by coexisting. Introduced to the kitchen, this concept is a stimulus to seek a mixture of ingredients as in the field. I see *la milpa* as a metaphor of life, an example of simplicity and integration, a way for optimizing resources without waste, like chapulinas, grasshoppers that instead of being exterminated chemically are gathered, cooked, and served at the table. They are excellent.

Mexican cooking often has a stereotyped image abroad, muddled and mixed up with U.S. Tex-Mex. Olvera's cooking and experimentation, inspired by ancient cultivation techniques and old recipes, work in the opposite direction. In the same interview with *Slow*, he spoke about the gem of his culinary repertoire:

Foreigners think that the distinctive elements of Mexican gastronomy are maize and beans. They are forgetting about plantains, which are boiled, fried, and grilled, and served on their own or with rice, sugar, and tortilla, as an appetizer or as a dessert. I wanted to recover a flavor of my childhood that has now been lost; the "rotten" plantain I used to eat at my grandma's house. Fermented flavors are an important element in Mexican cooking and are cited by Italo Calvino in his short story collection *Under the Jaguar Sun*, inspired by a trip to Oaxaca. We tried maturing the plantains for about 20 days and frying them in butter. The result is a sort of crème with the consistency of foie gras that goes very well with sour cream, spices, cacao, and grated macadamia nuts. It isn't sweet because the sugars in the fruit turn to alcohol, and the combination of acid and fat make it a perfect entrée.

One only has to browse through the monumental oeuvre of José Iturriaga de la Fuente, a distinguished historian and economist who has written an impressive range of studies and collected a huge number of indigenous recipes, to understand that the possibilities for a creative, sensitive cook may be never-ending. For example, on the Gulf of Mexico they use many species of wild animal in the kitchen: deer, boar, squirrels, iguanas, ducks. One thing that we are completely unaware of is the frequent use Mexicans make of roots and tubers, such as the sweet potato. Twenty or so edible flowers—*biznaga*, agave, *huauzontle*, *alache*, *hueynacastle*, to name just a few—are used to flavor dishes. It is not easy to imagine how important insects are as a source of profit for those who still know how to catch them: in the states of Chiapas and Veracruz, for example, the catching of *chicatanas*, flying ants, is a motive of collective celebration for the community, while the *gusano de maguey*, or agave grub, is often seen in the bottom of bottles of mescal, though I can assure you that it is also delicious fried.

With its allusions to its ancestral origins, to agriculture, to its food products, and with its promise of new evolutions in the future, gastronomy is doing its bit for the Mexican liberation process. It is spurring a liberation that will bring emancipation from the excessive power of the market, hence Mexicans are embracing its political demands. Many social and political movements have sprung up to ask governments to show greater awareness toward the environment, sustainable agriculture, and the weakest sections of the population.

Young people, too, have entered the arena with great energy. On May 11, 2012, the then presidential candidate Enrique Peña Nieto was heckled during a meeting at the Universidad Iberoamericana on account of the violence of his security personnel following a demonstration by flower sellers in 2007, when he was governor of the State of Mexico. His response so angered the students that he had to escape from the university by a back door.

The leading Mexican television networks and newspapers were quick to play down the protests, arguing that they had been organized not by the students but by the opposition party, the Partido de la Revolución Democrática.

Following this media stand, 131 students posted a video on YouTube in which they displayed their university ID cards and reiterated that they had taken part in the protest. The agitation subsequently spilled over onto the social networks, where other students and citizens began to back the protest, using the hashtag #YoSoy132 to identify with the 132nd student, and to show their intention of going ahead with it.

The Yo Soy 132 Manifesto, published on May 23, 2012, begins as follows:

The current situation in Mexico demands its youth to take over the current issues. It is time for us, the youth, to fight for a change in our country. It is time to strive for a Mexico with more freedom, more prosperity, and more justice. We want the current situation of misery, inequality, and violence to be resolved. We, the Mexican youth, believe that the current political and economic system does not respond to the demands of all Mexicans.

The document continues with a long list of demands, at the top of which is that for a radical change in the existing neoliberal economic system. The Mexican people want to take control of their own present to move in the direction of change, and no gas-tronome can pull out of the process because the food system is already an integral part of it. Food is central.

# CHAPTER 5

# COLOMBIA, THE IMPORTANCE OF THE LAND

To speak of gastronomy, especially of the gastronomy of liberation, is to speak, above all, of the land. Not only for the obvious reason that food preparation always begins with a fruit of the soil, but, most of all, because, as I have had the opportunity to point out on other occasions, if it is to be "good, clean, and fair," food requires equitable management of the land and respect for the people who work it.

If we are to continue to speak about community agriculture, communities themselves must be guaranteed access to the land and the chance to work it freely, democratically, and with dignity. Here I am not playing with words: the concrete need to solve the problem is more urgent and pressing than ever.

In many countries, the land is still at the center of bloody, age-old disputes whose resolutions still seem far off. As we have seen, there is no shortage of virtuous examples in Latin America, but there are countries in which the process has yet to be completed and which give us a better understanding of exactly what is at stake. One of these is Colombia, where the conflict between government forces and the guerillas of FARC, Fuerzas Armadas Revolucionarias de Colombia, has been going on for almost sixty years. The causes of the hostilities, which have grown jaundiced over the decades, are largely rooted in the fundamental question of land distribution. The conflict began in the field and the bases of peace have to be laid in the field.

Historically, after the Spanish colonial period, the land in Colombia gradually became the property of a few, indeed a very few, people. Following the armed conquest of the land, first by large ranch owners (often with private militias at their service) and later by criminal drugs gangs, many indigenous and Afro-American rural communities were forced to abandon their places of origin and land and live virtually as *deplazados*, deportees.

It is no coincidence that, before they lapsed into gratuitous violence and organized drug trafficking, the guerilla formations listed the demands of peasants among their main objectives.

Slowly but inexorably, monocultures, especially oil palms, replaced native crops, reducing food sovereignty and wiping entire peasant communities off the map, often with the blessing of the World Bank and the United Nations Development Program.

During the past year, after fifty years of nonstop conflict, peace negotiations were launched for the umpteenth time, with the question of the land and peasant rights still high on the agenda. The future of a country, Colombia, which despite the ongoing state of insecurity is the third largest economy in South America, will depend on the management of the land and agrarian reform.

At the start of 2013, FARC, the main Colombian guerrilla group and the government's negotiating partner, drew up a document containing ten points on which it intends to prod the government vis-à-vis the rural question. They range from implementation of agrarian reform for land redistribution to the regulation of the right of access to land, from the elimination of hunger to the fight against inequality and the recognition of the state's historic political, economic, social, and cultural debt toward the countryside. This debt, claims the FARC negotiating document, "has produced violence, exclusion, inequality, poverty, discrimination, and territorial segregation." To cite one figure documented by the Centro Nacional de Memoria Histórica, in the last fifty years of the conflict, 177,307 people died and 25,077 disappeared. The vast majority of them were peasants.

We too often tend to think that the question of the land has lost its central relevance. The opposite is true, as the Colombian situation, the disgraceful land grabbing that is afflicting Africa, and devastating, unstoppable, uncontrolled building in Europe testify. The land and the use that is made of it remain the linchpins for the building of society and the civil community, and as an essential basis for any informed debate about gastronomy.

It is not only a matter of distributing property and regulating access. Also fundamental is the idea of land use underlying the discussions. In a country as rich in resources as Colombia, the number of open mines, for example, is continuing to grow, and mining concessions have erased whole communities. Ecosystems are menaced by a productive use of natural resources oriented to profit for the sake of profit.

The mining industry, on one hand, and large landowners, on the other, who line their pockets with the profits from monocultures for export (oil palms, sugarcane, coffee), have transformed a country that, at the start of the 1990s, was virtually self-sufficient in terms of food into the Colombia of today, which produces just 50 percent of its inhabitants' food requirement.

According to a study by the Colombian Rural Development Institute, INCODER (Instituto Colombiano de Desarollo Rural), an agency that responds to the Ministry of Agriculture, Colombia is the country in the world with the greatest inequality of land distribution, with 1.1 percent of the population possessing 53.2 percent. In the course of the conflict, 6.6 hectares of land were expropriated from smallholders and almost 5 million people were forced to move to towns and cities. There are, moreover, 22 million hectares of arable land in Colombia, but only 5.3 million are used for agriculture, while of the 15.2 million hectares of pastureland only 3.5 million are used. To complete the picture, 5.8 million hectares of land are exploited by the mining industry. The figure is eloquent in its simplicity: it shows that more land is dedicated to mining than to farming and that resources are distributed very unequally.

Any exhaustive gastronomic discourse has to set out from here; if it fails to do so, it will lead nowhere. This is a political question of capital importance, because to deprive a people of its food sovereignty is to negate the right to food enshrined in the Universal Declaration of Human Rights in 1948. A country that destroys its rural fabric in the name of market speculation is a country that puts its own future at risk. It is no coincidence that the INCODER study cited above evidences how 70 percent of the food produced and consumed in Colombia comes from 800,000 farms with an average area of three hectares. Is any more evidence needed to understand that small-scale farmers are the only people capable of supplying a nation with adequate food resources? Unfortunately, it is.

May 15, 2012, saw the entry into force of the United States–Colombia Free Trade Agreement which, according to the governments of the two countries, would finally allow Colombian products to access the vast U.S. market, free from customs complications and duties. But the agreement soon showed itself for what it really was: a way of hoodwinking smallholders and favoring the large landowners and industrial farms (this latter is an oxymoron I use to define those who practice industrial agriculture on a large scale). The arrival of mostly government-subsidized U.S. agro-industrial products on the Colombian market is bringing peasant farmers, unable to compete pricewise, to their knees. It may be useful to cite one statistic in particular to give a sense of the magnitude of the phenomenon: in 2006, Colombia was importing 9,727 tons of dairy products, but in 2012, the year the Free Trade Agreement came into force, the figure increased to 33,728. The people who paid for this were, of course, Colombian dairy breeders.

In the summer of 2013, street protests broke out in a number of Colombian towns and cities, with students, workers, academics, and citizens of every social extraction going on the warpath alongside peasant farmers. If work in the fields is not decently remunerated, there is no future for agriculture, for gastronomy, or for food sovereignty.

In Colombia, too, gastronomy is being liberated, but there liberation will depend more than elsewhere on the land. The support the Colombian people are giving their peasant farmers is the greatest seed of hope for a more just future. As gastronomes, we have no other option but to take a stand, conscious of the role that the discipline we have chosen imposes upon us in the ongoing debate. We are at the side of peasant farmers who demand dignity for their labor and a future for their families; we are at the side of anyone who is close to the land.

# CHAPTER 6

# PROSPECTS FOR NEW LIBERATIONS ACROSS THE ATLANTIC

**W**hat is happening in Latin America on the front of gastronomy, in the fullest meaning of the term, is extraordinary. For the first time in history, in a place that is not Europe, it is precisely gastronomy that is becoming a protagonist at the center of epoch-making change. It is not surprising that almost all the actors I have mentioned—be they chefs or humble peasant farmers, producers' associations or educators, communicators, students, or militants—plus all the many others who I have not yet had the good fortune to meet, always use the word gastronomy to describe what they are doing. They are all perfectly conscious that, whatever their own specific activity, they are all part of a broad, unstructured, "liquid" movement, that their actions and practices are part of something much larger, a network of complex relations unforeseeable but aimed at a single goal: redemption.

Here I have spoken about the situation in Colombia without exploring the disasters wreaked by the multinationals elsewhere in Latin America, the vast expanses of GM soybeans, the daylight robbery that is the patentability of seeds and active principles of many vegetable varieties for medical purposes, the violence against peasant farmers, the destruction of forests, the irreparable alteration of ecosystems.

However you look at it, it is a truly desolate picture, which is why I have preferred to concentrate on the positive side of things and the ferment coming out of Latin America. The power of the malign forces at work is overwhelming compared to that of the network of people and communities that are recovering skills and food products and rediscovering their multiform roots to write the story of their future and their land. It is undeniable, however, that we are witnessing a rebirth—or maybe it would be more correct to say birth—which is beginning to develop and to liberate energy to oppose these forces, born of new paradigms and, above all, of a holistic conception of gastronomic knowledge.

From this point of view, it is interesting to note a convergence of ambitions and ideals, planned by no one, but very widespread and very transversal. This common sensibility promises great things for the future. Opposed, conflicting ideas will continue to coexist, but we will not be seeing the total triumph of multinational industry and unsustainable systems of production and consumption. Elements of biodiversity and a unique wealth of material culture ensure a new perspective as part of a process favored by economic development that is affecting, with varying degrees of intensity but always positively, the whole of Latin America. The liberation of energies, which I mentioned when I was speaking about networks and which is taking place in the BRIC and CIVETS countries, also envisages the possibility of restaurants with high prices, inaccessible to the majority—but vital in driving change—and in any case the creation of a general well-being that allows new forms of entrepreneurship and commitment in the ambit of gastronomy.

However, I believe that the "ideological" results the phenomenon is achieving in Central and South America, fully in tune with the ideas of Slow Food and Terra Madre, really can extend to any region of the world seeking redemption from poverty. And that it can lead in other areas to progressive liberations, thereby justifying our total commitment to eradicating the scourge of hunger and malnutrition everywhere using gastronomy as one of the tools. Our network is a continuing source of encouragement; in certain African communities, for example, I see the seeds of the same type of change and I am convinced that sooner or later liberation will spread to Africa, too.

The most positive aspect of the question is that Africans are perfectly equipped to set the same process into motion. For in Africa, too, gastronomy is proving an extraordinary key, especially if you have the good fortune to be acquainted with the communities and realities of Slow Food and Terra Madre. I have already mentioned a few examples, such as Lare in Kenya, home to a presidium and a restaurant. Yet Terra Madre in Africa has liberated something even greater, giving birth with the tiniest cues to a new network perfectly capable of growing and expanding on its own. I found this out for myself on a trip to Uganda in 2012. There we have already gone far beyond the targets we set ourselves, and the terrain is fertile for a gastronomic revolution analogous to the one in Latin America in the most diverse realities of Africa.

Crossing the Kenya-Uganda border at Malaba in April 2012, I was welcomed by Frederick Wabusima, better known as Freddy, a popular broadcaster on the local STEP TV network. Thanks to his radio programs, schools and associations in eastern Uganda have been acquainted with Slow Food's presence and projects in the country, like the Thousand Gardens in Africa. Freddie is also a convivium leader and a Terra Madre delegate and, working entirely as volunteer, has developed the Slow Food movement around the city of Mbale. With him was Baker Ssenyondwa, a member of Slow Food who kindly volunteered to be my driver on my journey through Uganda.

They took me first of all to see two school gardens—one at the St. Stephen Secondary School in Bupoto, the other at the nursery school in Bunanimi—both part of the Thousand Gardens in Africa project. At the St. Stephen Secondary School I was welcomed by a small but comprehensive exhibition of local biodiversity. The show they put on was amazing, with dozens and dozens of varieties of fruits, vegetables, cereals, and tubers on display on the desks in the schoolyard, many wild, others cultivated in the school garden and by the villagers—a remarkable bounty. They described to me the processing and preparation techniques for local dishes, showing me how protecting these varieties, mostly unfamiliar to the European visitor, was indispensable to keep local gastronomic identities alive, besides ensuring a minimal decent level of food security.

To say that first impact with Uganda was illuminating would be a euphemism. The Bunanimi Primary School that I visited immediately afterward was even more of a revelation, but I shall reveal why only after first recounting my memory of the journey as a whole. The potentialities that emerge from that experience are among the founding elements of my conviction that gastronomy is the right way for Africa, that the free network holds surprises in store, that the fight against hunger and malnutrition is not a utopia, but is feasible and credible, something for which it is necessary to join forces all over the world, not without changing points of view first. It will be necessary to place unconditional faith in local forces and their way of interpreting gastronomic science, supporting them and letting them do the work they know and which they cannot wait to begin.

# CHAPTER 7

# UGANDA, A VIEW OF THE FUTURE

The day after my arrival in Uganda, traveling from Mbale to the capital Kampala, I was able to see some of the many different faces of the country. We set off early and by mid-morning we had reached Jinja, a colonial town that had sprung up on the shores of Lake Victoria to house the thousands of Indians British colonialists brought to eastern Africa to work on the building of the Kenya-Uganda railway. It was those Indians who imported the chapati, now the principal table bread in this portion of Africa, a testimony to the power of syncretism and the formation of new identities. Jinja is situated at the exact point where the Nile leaves the lake to follow its over 6,000 kilometer course through five different countries. Just out of town, the Kampala road cuts through the luxuriant Mabira Forest like a knife, slicing it in two. The forest is the pride of the whole country, its green lung, and is home to a great many endemic species and rural communities, which, over the centuries, have developed a symbiotic relationship with its resources to be able to have food to eat. Some representatives of these communities have been to Terra Madre and are part of the network.

Unfortunately, the sense of marvel we felt seeing the two sheer green walls and the monkeys climbing up them soon disappeared. At a certain point, after a few kilometers, the forest came to a sudden end and the landscape changed completely; now low-lying sugar and tea plantations stretched out as far as the eye could see. The Ugandan government has sold off huge portions of the forest for large Indian corporations to convert them into cultivable land. This is one of the most common forms of land grabbing but, disconcertingly, African governments often mistake it for a development opportunity. The forest has literally disappeared to leave way to industrial monocultures, which produce the tea and sugar we consume for breakfast every morning. I cannot imagine what the communities that inhabited these vast swaths of land must have gone through. They were probably driven away without having any choice in the matter, maybe under threat. The ecosystem, which was essential for their survival, has been completely destroyed. Who knows where they have gone? Here, unfortunately, there are no land registers as we know them and, without the possibility of legal aid, people can be uprooted from the place where they and their ancestors have always lived, plowed, hunted, and gathered. This is land grabbing, but also life grabbing.

That afternoon, after arriving in Kampala, the capital, on the shores of Lake Victoria, I delivered a lecture at the prestigious Makerere University. It was attended by all the Slow Food Uganda convivium leaders and a large number of members. I had been invited to speak by Professor Moses Makooma-Tenywa, a lecturer at the Agriculture Department, where his team has developed a revolutionary application known as the Open Distance Learning Network, whereby information about agricultural prices and techniques are loaded in audio format on a computer that acts as a central server. For some years now, by dialing a number on their mobile phones (in the evening, when calls are free under special contract conditions formulated by Ugandan telephone companies), smallholders can listen to news, including instructions on how to plant one of Slow Food's Thousand Gardens in Africa. In a short space of time, mobile phones have become the most important form of personal communication in Africa, performing functions unknown to or unused by us, such as the payment of bills and shopping and money transfers by a simple text message. This is a little big innovation that allows money to circulate more easily, thus improving the economic growth rate in many countries. The system invented by Professor Makooma-Tenywa uses new technologies and is capable of networking the most remote rural communities in Uganda, disseminating modern and sustainable cultivation techniques, and publishing prices to connect producers with consumers and promote fairer trade. The service also makes use of text messages and radio bulletins. Thanks to the team of researchers coordinated by Professor Makooma-Tenywa, most of whom are Slow Food members, the Slow Food philosophy has managed to penetrate everywhere in the country, generating important possibilities for agriculturalists. When they visited Terra Madre, the Makerere University team caught the Slow Food bug and went home to expand the movement in Uganda in a way that we in Bra found hard to believe.

Our meeting at the university ended with an impressively vibrant speech by a young man called Edward Mukiibi, better known as Edie, a convivium leader and Terra Madre delegate. That was the first time I had met him and he followed me for all the rest of the journey. Today Edie is one of the new members of the Slow Food International Council and the International Board of Directors, which, composed of just six people and with executive powers, is the association's most important body. The impetus he has brought to the coordination of the network, the development of projects, and the spreading of the ideas of Slow Food and Terra Madre in Uganda has been so strong as to make expansion there one of Slow Food International's top priorities. The most impressive feature of all this progress—above all, for anybody tempted to stick to the commonplace notion that cooperation projects in Africa can only be achieved with aid from wealthy foreign countries and subjects—is that almost everything they have done, they have done with their own resources on their own initiative without recourse to external funding, but showing creativity and exploiting the potential of the network to the full. During the meeting in Istanbul in June 2013, in a submeeting of groups of representatives divided by continents, other African Slow Food International Council members asked who and how to ask for more resources, and Edie replied by citing his own work:

> We exploit personal relations, above all. We don't ask ourselves who might give us money, we try to find alternative solutions. I know Professor Moses and I try to spread our initiatives with text messages and bulletins on the university telephone . . . not everyone can do this, at least without paying. I know Freddy who talks on the radio, and I get him to broadcast our messages on air, we have developed friendships and collaborations with some people who work in television and we have our messages broadcast free. It costs us nothing, we've simply tried to exploit the potential of our Ugandan network to the full.

Any further comment would be superfluous.

My tour of Uganda proceeded over the next few days with a visit to Luweero for the inauguration of a new Slow Food Presidium, the first in Uganda and the first anywhere to be dedicated to robusta coffee, old varieties of which have been cultivated in the district for a very long time. Uganda is famous the world over for its production of robusta, which is used largely to add body to espresso coffee blends with the more aromatic arabica variety. Though the Ugandan government is pushing everywhere to replace traditional varieties with more productive commercial hybrids, in Luweero many growers have preferred to preserve the ancient varieties, which are more disease resistant, and also delicious. We went to the house of Ernest Kigozi, a farmer and a community leader. The place was surrounded by very rare old coffee plants, some of them fifty years old, all tall and robust, there to celebrate the new presidium dedicated to *kiboko*. *Kiboko* is the most common Ugandan term for coffee and derives from the name of the stick British colonialists would use to punish lazy growers who forgot to turn over coffee berries drying in the sun. At the inauguration of the presidium, we made a toast with a coffee traditionally prepared according to a ritual procedure involving the removal of the flesh from the beans, pre-toasting in an iron skillet, toasting in an earthenware pot, and grinding in a mortar. The coffee powder infused in the water gave me taste sensations I had never experienced before, and the beverage was better than any regular espresso drinker could ever imagine. The "ritual" was shared by a packed crowd of producers from the new presidium, they too keen to wave their flags with the Slow Food snail symbol. For them, in fact, the initiative at last means finding the proper, decently remunerated commercial outlets for their product, promoted for its gastronomic value and not only at generally over-low, or precariously oscillating, internationally fixed prices.

My last day in Uganda was again dedicated to school gardens, this time in the districts of Mukono and Kayunga on the outskirts of Kampala. Accompanied by members of the Slow Food Mukono convivium, a group of youngsters who have translated the principles of "good, clean, and fair" at the local level, I visited three schools. At the last, a party had been organized in collaboration with the leaders of the taste education projects, not in my honor but to respect a tradition that has been repeated for some time now at the end of each school year. At the Buiga Sunrise Primary School, I was welcomed by an army of small children in red and yellow uniforms, red and yellow being Uganda's national colors. A Fruit&Juice party was in full flow, with the children and their families having a great time promoting the consumption of local fresh fruit and its by-products among the rural population. The fruit was so sweet and juicy, it was as if I had never eaten fruit in my life before. At the party I also had the pleasure of meeting another great ally of the Slow Food Mukono convivium, the Dembe catering group, a team of female cooks, also members of the Terra Madre network, that passes on the secrets of Ugandan cooking to children in the central districts of Uganda. They use gastronomy and cooking as training tools, teaching sensory education and reviving local diets and recipes. They are one of the pillars of Slow Food projects in Uganda. By explaining the recipes of tradition to children, and hence to their parents who had lost them in the first place, gastronomy is achieving small liberations that are a manna for many an ailing family economy. It is ensuring healthy, nourishing food that is easy to find, easy to grow, and easy to cook.

The Bunanimi Primary School, the one I promised I would return to, is very different from the other schools we visited on the first day of the journey. Public, not private, it is attended by the children of the poorest sections of the population in one of the most difficult, problematic areas of Uganda. It is also home to another of the Thousand Gardens in Africa. When, on my arrival, I saw a slogan in huge block capital letters on the roof warning pupils not to accept gifts in return for sexual favors, my blood froze. The schoolyard was parched and dusty. On the way there, I had seen what life was like in this area, where families work sparse plots of land around their very humble dwellings. When the harvest is richer than normal—which is rarely—it is nonetheless still hard to sell produce. Money is scarce, the people are excluded from the economy, and all they eat is what they manage to grow.

On that occasion, the pupils were accompanied by their parents. The whole bunch of them, children and adults, were seated in the schoolyard waiting for me. We were slightly late because the roads had been bad, and we had had problems with the car. The parents' presence was a signal that the school performs a vitally important social function that transcends its educational one. The garden, in fact, serves not only to educate the children, but also entire communities. The parents are totally involved in the horticultural project and the communities play an active part, producing and exchanging seeds and swapping growing techniques. The pupils take home the seeds they have multiplied in the garden, and thus allow their families to diversify the varieties they sow and reproduce the same crops at home. The garden thus acts as a link between the culture produced inside the school and the knowledge incorporated in the traditional skills of which rural African communities are repositories. At these latitudes, reinforcing the diversity of crops signifies reducing the vulnerability of families menaced by food insecurity. Teaching how to cultivate a garden may lead to salvation. Bunanimi was a significant stage on my first day in Uganda. I had only been in the country for a few hours, but already I had seen what Terra Madre can do—and what gastronomy can do—for liberation. The tools that can be used are as numerous as the crops, areas, and starting conditions, and when they are managed at the grassroots level by people under their own steam and according to their own traditions, they work well and they work lastingly. Of these tools, the garden is not only a symbol, it is also a harbinger of real change.

# CHAPTER 8

# TEN THOUSAND GARDENS IN AFRICA

At Salone del Gusto–Terra Madre in Turin in 2012, it was possible to leave the stands in the four pavilions of the Lingotto Fiere exhibition complex and walk through a long tunnel lined by stalls of steaming street food to the Oval, a structure built for the short track skating events at the Turin 2006 Winter Olympics. Today the Oval is part of the exhibition complex and we have made use of it for the last two Salone del Gusto–Terra Madre events. In 2012, it housed the Slow Food international presidia and their producers, including many from the Terra Madre food communities, which for the first time in the history of the event had stands and a market of their own.

To the rear of the Oval, virtually at the end of an ideal tour of the Salone, visitors were pleasantly surprised to find a whole section dedicated to Africa: at the center of the area, 400 square meters of floor space was covered with soil to create a large African garden. It was possible to observe all sorts of plants and walk past rows of strange beans and eggplants never seen before in Italy. There were varieties of leafy vegetables (in Africa they eat the leaves of potatoes, pumpkins, amaranth, and manioc) and medicinal herbs, such as vetiver, used to repel harmful insects. There was a seedbed and there were explanations of how to intercrop two different plants to mutual benefit, which systems of fertilization to adopt to avoid using chemicals, how to irrigate without expensive equipment by following methods ancient (such as perforated earthenware jars) and modern (such as recycled plastic bottles hanging from a line). The fences were made not with netting or cement, but with the materials usually found around any African garden: branches, palm and bamboo leaves, thorny bushes. It was a perfect large-scale reproduction, an educational garden that explained to visitors the work that is being done in many African communities on small plots of land with plants, fruit trees, and compost heaps. The garden was international because it represented the crops of all twenty-five countries involved in the Thousand Gardens in Africa project.

It is true that the Turin garden combined crops and techniques that could not coexist in nature (it took us months to import all the plants and, with the precious help of a Piedmontese nurseryman, get them ready for the event) for reasons of latitude and season. But we felt the exceptional anomaly was justified by the importance of explaining to visitors to Salone del Gusto–Terra Madre the wealth of biodiversity of the African continent, and of creating gardens in communities and schools, such as Bunanimi, Buiga Sunrise, or St. Stephen in Uganda, or in Kenya at the primary school in Michinda in the Elburgon hills. This latter project has been underway since 2005 and, thanks to the enterprise of Samuel Muhunyu, a Kenyan delegate at Terra Madre in 2004, now the heart and soul of the movement in his country and a member of the Slow Food International Council, was one of the first to be funded by Slow Food.

This garden, cultivated on a voluntary basis by the school's four hundred pupils, has been voted the best in Kenya. Here the children had to overcome the skepticism of their parents, who did not want them to get involved because in Kenya, as in other African countries, working in the garden has always been seen as a way of punishing unruly pupils. But given the project's sensational success, now even the most skeptical parents are proud of it. I still carry in my heart the memory of the party laid on for me by the children at Michinda —all proud, super-qualified farmers—and I still wear the scarf they gave me. The same scarf, incidentally, played a starring role at Salone del Gusto–Terra Madre 2012, where I held it up as a symbol of our new project for the gastronomy of liberation (though I still had not invented the term!).

Today the Thousand Gardens in Africa really do exist. In just less than two years since 2011, we have planted 20 in Morocco, Mauritania (one of which is inside a UN refugee camp), Egypt, Madagascar, the Democratic Republic of Congo; 30 in Burkina Faso and Mozambique; 35 in Ethiopia; 40 in Tanzania, Senegal, and the Ivory Coast; 60 in Sierra Leone and Mali; 70 in Guinea Bissau; 75 in Uganda; 150 in South Africa; and as many as 200 in Kenya; plus others in Tunisia, Somalia, Gabon, Cameroon, Benin, Ghana, Cape Verde, and Malawi. These are not just any gardens; they are planted by the communities themselves and they valorize the capabilities of all their members, from the elderly to the young, not to mention local technicians. The gardens do not require a large amount of space and are planted wherever it is possible, sometimes in the most unlikely places such as rooftops or pathways. They are gardens of biodiversity because they grow local varieties, some of which are in danger of extinction, and hardy nutritional varieties that do not need to be treated with chemicals. The seeds are multiplied and managed by the communities themselves with sustainable agro-ecological techniques and using water sparingly. The gardens have an educational function for children and for the whole community and, above all, they are interconnected by the Terra Madre network, where a group oversees exchanges of seeds and skills and travels to share advice. A very detailed instruction manual to teach people how to develop the gardens, much appreciated by the communities and Slow Food representatives, has been compiled and translated into all the relevant languages.

So what have we done in Bra? Nothing other than mobilize and, through our association (many convivia around the world, especially in Italy, have "adopted" a garden), raise the 900 euros necessary to finance each single project, to buy the few tools required and carry out the preparation and management work. The communities themselves have done all the rest. At our headquarters in Bra we have a small office where technicians have also helped a great deal by training national coordinators, of which there are now over fifty in the whole of Africa who travel to connect communities and help them start up. We have calculated that school and community gardens (as we have seen, the difference between the two is minimal) involve 30,000 people (women, men, children, farmers, teachers, cooks) who grow and water and harvest them.

The success of the project has been so rapid and so total—with the added advantage that, since 2004, it has expanded our network in places where Slow Food did not even exist—as to wrong-foot the people who had looked at me as if I were punch-drunk, carried away by my umpteenth utopia, when I told them of my scheme for a thousand gardens in Africa. So what did I do? I decided to launch the third of the "three ten thousands" that I mentioned in previous chapters, during the last Slow Food international congress in Turin: through the entire Slow Food–Terra Madre network, the planting of 10,000 gardens in Africa by 2016. After achieving one objective, we multiplied it by ten—talk about "unpairing the cards"!

The picture of the "three ten thousands" is now complete: 10,000 food products for loading on the Ark of Taste; 10,000 nodes in the network; 10,000 gardens in Africa. The program, as you have read, follows a course in which the objectives are at once tools and values, are connected, feed one another, and aim to achieve liberation by using liberated gastronomy. The "Ten Thousand Gardens in Africa" project is the most "strategic" part of the whole. My personal experiences, but also those of all my collaborators who run the association in Africa (a few Italians at the international headquarters in Bra and the Africans in their own countries), have opened my eyes and convinced members of Slow Food and Terra Madre in other continents to support this revolutionary new action with all their force. Africa is becoming the focus of all our efforts, because it represents the future and is showing why. It is, in fact, the place in the world where hunger and malnutrition are one of the most dramatic problems, but exist alongside traditions, resources, biodiversity, skills, cultures, and lands that—if they have not been plundered by colonizers of every type, if they have not been homogenized or erased by a form of progress that has gone in the wrong direction for too long, creating more problems than solutions—will become the wealth on which the future of the world can be built, not just that of Africa. They can become an example, the tool to eradicate from the face of the earth once and for all the scourge of hunger and malnutrition, the disgrace of our civilization, with which too many people continue to live without doing a thing, many without even thinking about it or knowing what to do.

A garden provides food to eat, is sustainable, is a vehicle for food culture, allows the practice of traditional gastronomy. It also provides food for thought and stimulates the creativity of young people so they can invent new ways of redemption, and restores dignity to the elders who take part with their wisdom. This is happening in Africa, but also in Central and South America, in

Europe, in North America, in Asia, and in Oceania, in urban, school, and rural community gardens, in poor countries as in rich countries. For malnutrition is present in rich countries, too. The ongoing crisis, in fact, is plunging many families and many of our city dwellers under the poverty threshold; they are often hidden but they are there and there are many of them. A gastronome cannot remain indifferent. We can and we must set out from Africa to liberate the world from hunger and famine. We can and we must join forces in this battle for civilization, from which no one can be excluded. Latin America has already pointed to a possible way and it is not far-fetched to think that Africa can find a way of its own. In the globalized world, that would be a benefit for everyone. Mark my words: if we all do our bit, each in his or her own geographical context, we can make it happen.

# CHAPTER 9

# ALL TOGETHER AGAINST THE DISGRACE OF HUNGER AND MALNUTRITION

In the Bible, the two great misfortunes of the Hebrew people were hunger and slavery, and the holy book tells us how they were liberated from both. Joseph regenerated granaries to save his people from hunger and Moses rescued them from slavery. In 1926, the League of Nations, the forerunner of the United Nations, suppressed the slave trade and slavery in all its member countries. The relevant convention laid a tombstone over a practice as old as the history of humanity, which still continued nonetheless (the last country to abolish slavery was Mauritania, as late as 1980) and in subtler, more devious forms probably still does, albeit marginally. History speaks of the great victory of abolitionism, the political movement that came into being in the late eighteenth century, which succeeded in erasing a scandal that lasted in the "civilized" United States of America until 1865, when the end of the Civil War also saw the passing of the Thirteenth Amendment. It took three centuries to cancel the word slavery from the daily practice of other countries, too. It was a great victory, the fruit of a widespread international movement born of the Enlightenment in an age in which moral and humanitarian demands were starting to be broadly shared.

When I speak of liberations, I am also speaking about slavery: its abolition—the milestones of which were the Thirteenth Amendment in the United States in 1865 and the 1926 League of Nations Convention—was a historic event that set the seal on a change in paradigm. Humanity had tolerated this iniquitous practice since the dawn of time, considering it an uncomfortable necessity for purposes that were evidently and merely economic. At one point, however, what had previously been tolerated became intolerable, and today anyone would be appalled if its reintroduction were broached.

Returning to the two biblical scourges, it is clear that the process of their elimination has yet to be completed, that the paradigm has to go further. Why is no one appalled today by the statistics on hunger and malnutrition? What would it take to form a popular international movement to fight this scourge, tolerated by almost everyone on the planet the way slavery used to be tolerated? We find ourselves in the same situation as the United States at the time of Lincoln: on the one hand, a Declaration of Independence hinged on equality among human beings; on the other, a state that banks its fortunes on the inequality of slaves. The right to food has been established by the charters of international bodies, yet almost a billion people suffer for the lack of it. The time has come to say enough is enough, to unite our forces and work for another historic triumph in the name of universal rights. And, insofar as the subject is food, gastronomes have to be at the forefront. We have to free ourselves from hunger and malnutrition.

The document drawn up for the Slow Food International Congress (which I wrote with Carlo Bogliotti, Rinaldo Rava, and Cinzia Scaffidi) sets out the guidelines for the movement from 2012 to 2016. Entitled *The Central Role of Food*, it is divided into three parts: "About us," "What we are talking about," and "What we are doing." The second deals with the "right to food" and demonstrates how the gastronomic battle is above all a battle for civilization. The first section speaks very clearly:

> To say that food has to become a central element of our thinking about people again is to say something eminently political. That of food consumers is a "non-category" insofar as actions targeted at food consumers are targeted at all humanity. This is why they are political actions par excellence.
>
> Nowadays we think of consumers as people who "buy" food, but if food concerns us only insofar as it is sold and bought (thus becoming a competence of economic policy and not of politics as such), then we lose sight of food as a right. Yet that which is essential for survival is part of the sphere of rights: this is why we speak of the right to food and the right to water.
>
> Ever since it was formulated in Article 11 of the International Covenant on Economic, Social and Cultural rights adopted by the General Assembly of the United Nations in 1966, the idea of the right to food has been accompanied by the right to freedom from hunger.
>
> Point 1 of Article 11 asserts "the right of everyone to an adequate standard of living for himself and his family, including adequate food, clothing and housing, and to

the continuous improvement of living conditions," while point 2 recognizes "the fundamental right of everyone to be free from hunger."

Without this second point, Article 11 would not raise such pressing questions. Its choice of words should make us stop and think. It speaks of freedom from hunger, because hunger is a form of slavery, above all physical slavery, that may translate into social and economic slavery, often involving the very governments of countries that are slaves to hunger, in which case it becomes political slavery.

This is why our movement has to declare a fight against hunger [ . . . ] There is something else in Article 11 of the UN Covenant that attracts our attention: the point which speaks about the "continuous improvement" of living conditions. We have to ask ourselves whether there is a limit to that "continuous improvement" and what the concept of limit actually means. Do those who have achieved the guarantee of the right to food and freedom from hunger have the right to improve themselves even though another part of humanity has yet to achieve that guarantee? Or do we reach a point at which the improvement of one compromises the right to food of another? It is the job of an association like ours to contribute to a review of the prospects of these rights. Because Slow Food protects the right to pleasure, and pleasure based on the suffering and slavery of others cannot exist [ . . . ] The dream of a life independent from the seasons and, more generally, from time and change, the utopia of freedom for many civilizations, was built on two main pillars: technical progress and money. Countries with enough technology would see their right to food ensured. The food industry and market-oriented industrial agriculture were the leading paladins of this vision. But a universal right closely connected to the very existence of humanity cannot be conditional. Without technology and money how can the right to food be guaranteed? [ . . . ] We have to wage a relentless war on starvation. There are no more urgent wars to be fought—there are no alternative priorities. We cannot speak about sustainability, about rights or about the future, if we do not speak, first and foremost, about hunger. Slow Food intends to take the battlefield without hesitation, fighting this war with no holds barred. FAO [Food and Agriculture Organization] estimates that it will take 34 billion dollars a year to reverse the trend once and for all—a ridiculous figure compared to the sums spent to bail European and American banks out of the financial crisis.

Thirty-four billion dollars a year is nothing for the world's economic powers. By way of comparison, an article published in the Italian daily newspaper *Il fatto quotidiano* in December 2012 declared that, "in spite of the precipice that has swallowed up the economies of the so-called 'developed' countries, the arms market continues to be stable, indeed it is growing. This harsh reality is photographed by SIPRI (the Stockholm International Peace Research Institute), in its international arms transfers database, updated to 2011. According to the data published by this independent agency the volume of conventional arms transfers increased in the period from 2007 to 2011 by 24 percent with respect to the previous five-year period (2002–2006) and amounts to 30 billion euros." At the exchange rate as I write, that is the equivalent of almost 40 billion euros. What is needed now is actions, not words.

One suspects that there is a precise interest in maintaining this state of affairs: an economic interest, as was the case with slavery. But before we start stirring the consciences of the mighty, before making hunger and malnutrition intolerable and having them expelled from our societies, before making everybody feel a deep sense of shame, we can begin by following the example of Latin America, of what has happened and is happening there. We can start planting gardens, ennobling gastronomy as a science of liberation, acting in local areas by avoiding waste, setting sustainable, virtuous dynamics into motion, and helping others near and far away in every way possible. We have to move together to repudiate a scandal that has no reason to exist in the twenty-first century. We have to vanquish this disgrace.

I have already listed the scandalous figures. There are still about a billion people who are starving in the world, a staggering number that varies little from one year to the next. One has the distinct sensation that, barring the situation we have described in Latin America, things will not change without a mobilization of consciences. A movement like Slow Food–Terra Madre has to engage in this battle as so many others around the world have done, FAO first and foremost (unsuccessfully, alas, though recent small inversions in trends provide some cause for hope). The problem is that the network of those involved has to extend to every living being, as have commitment and good practices.

Reading these assertions of mine, you may feel a sense of impotence and you may wonder how all this can be changed. I say that it is possible, if we create a movement capable of "unpairing the cards" on the world table and arguing that the right to food must be based on respect for small-scale agriculture and local gastronomies, on the right to water and the protection of biodiversity; a movement demanding that aid for urgent subsistence be overseen by a whole network of sub-movements, associations, groups of every religion and political color, and not only by the great international systems of governance. We must put all this forward, at last, as an element of true world liberation with a policy of integration, peace, valorization of cultural diversities, and the extraordinary innovative force that the young generations can bring. But we also have to come to terms with a very difficult historical reality in which, to cite just one example, wars show no sign of ceasing. I am nonetheless adamant that if everyone gives their all (which, in our case, means gastronomy), we will succeed in the intent sooner or later, even if it does take three centuries, as it did for slavery.

What it does not take to make ambitious projects happen is megastructures. What is important is to be conscious of one's limits and allow oneself to be regenerated by the people encountered on one's path. If I look back at our history, the history of Slow Food and Terra Madre, I see an evolution of content but also of many wonderful people, and it is my contention that they have all been fundamental—even if some of them have now moved in different directions. I will always admire the constant efforts of those who have had the courage to continue with us, and even of those who have not, to put themselves on the line. All of which leads me to believe that this last idea, which at first glance may seem overambitious, is not overambitious at all.

The important thing is to stick together, to never be alone. From now on, across the network, I will use and promote the slogan "Together we can make it happen." It will be translated into every language, and I personally will say it in my dialect, Piedmontese. My hope is that as the Italian words "*Terra Madre*" have become a patrimony of all of us all over the world, so *Tuti ansema podoma féila* can become a widely shared figure of speech, but, above all, of feeling. *Tuti ansema podoma féila* . . . Remember these words—the scandal has to come to an end!

# CHAPTER 10

# FOOD AND FREEDOM BECAUSE FOOD IS FREEDOM

*T*uti ansema podoma féila . . . I would like to end with two stories.

Ventanilla is a chaotic, dusty suburb of Lima, an area of stark cement houses on hills overlooking the Pacific Ocean, its dirt streets with no names fanning out without apparent order. It is very easy to get lost if you don't belong here, and people are used to giving directions to strangers looking for a particular place or address. After more than an hour of detours and U-turns in this neighborhood without vegetation (it hardly ever rains), we came to the Instituto de Cocina de Pachacutec, a cooking school housed in a complex just outside the center.

When I walked into the courtyard of the building one April afternoon, the Peruvian autumn sun was still beating down. I was accompanied by Gastón Acurio, whose Astrid y Gastón foundation funds some of the training activities. I have already spoken about Gastón, but thinking back to Ventanilla it is a pleasure to speak about him again. Every year thousands of students from almost every part of Peru apply to attend the program, but very rigorous selection and an admissions threshold system only allow about a hundred to actually enroll. To evaluate the eligibility of students, they take into account not only their skills and curricula, but also their socioeconomic background. The fact is that the Pachacutec school is another paradigmatic example of the gastronomy of liberation that has mushroomed in Peru over the last few years. The suburb of Ventanilla is poor but since 2007, the year it opened, the school has been a center of excellence that has offered totally new prospects—economic prospects included—for the young people who attend it.

Teachers of proven fame and great chefs are regular visitors to Pachacutec, bringing to the syllabus their professional expertise and gastronomic visions. Gastón, for example, has involved some of the big names in the international restaurant industry (one such, Ferran Adrià, inaugurated the school) and has used his charisma to forge important collaborations with other schools all over the world and restaurants all over South America. This allows students to acquire professional experience of the very highest level and to become acquainted with realities that would otherwise have been virtually beyond their reach. Motivation plays an important role in the program, whose backbone is the values of the new gastronomy of Latin American liberation. The school not only teaches top-flight culinary technique, but also dovetails it with knowledge of traditional Peruvian food products and ancestral indigenous dishes, with the emphasis on process sustainability and the cooks-farmers alliance.

Walking across the courtyard past the garden and through the kitchens and the classrooms, I had the chance to meet and chat briefly with some of the students. I asked them all to tell me why they had decided to become chefs. The replies I received turned on their heads the ones I had heard at Faculty of Gastronomic Science of the San Ignacio de Loyola University, where I had delivered a lecture earlier that morning. If at the university almost all the answers spoke of a vague, generic interest inspired by the success of top award-winning chefs and the proliferation of food and wine events the world over, at Pachacutec it was an entirely different kettle of fish. There I heard determined-looking kids of twelve to sixteen years of age use words like "desire to contribute to the family economy," "passion for my land's traditional foods," and "desire to find out what a people's gastronomic identity is." The gastronomy of liberation in a nutshell.

Culinary skills and knowledge of gastronomic culture offer these youngsters the prospect of professional and personal pride, of tangible self-fulfillment and achievement, and a unique opportunity for economic, social, and personal redemption.

The story that struck me the most was that of baby-faced Lucia, thirteen, who answered my question as follows, without hesitation, in an unwavering voice:

> I did everything I could to get into this school because I want to help my parents who are peasant farmers. I live in a suburb on the other side of town and it takes me three hours to get here. I have to walk part of the way, then take two buses. I do this every morning and every evening but it doesn't bother me because I know I can build a good future here for my family and me. They're peasants and they've always worked the land. We're poor but I know that, working as a cook, I can make them proud too by making the most of what they have done working the land all their lives. Here they teach us that every cook depends on the producers of primary ingredients and that you can't be a good cook if you aren't in close touch with peasants and farmers. This is why I'm totally committed to my studies and leaving home at half past four in the morning is just part of that commitment.

Lucia gets home every night at around eleven o'clock, but before she sets off she sweeps the school floors, though nobody asks her to. "For me the school is like a second home," she told me. Her words left me dumbstruck. I had never heard such a simple yet determined utterance in all my life.

This single-mindedness is the most important result of "liberated gastronomy," in turn the result of the liberation of diversity and the creation of a free network. It is the single-mindedness of those who know that a way exists for reconciling humanity with the soil and want to follow it in the best way possible, even in what are seemingly the most marginal contexts.

It is the way followed by Lucia Lantero and Agostino Terzi, two former students of the University of Gastronomic Sciences in Pollenzo who decided to embark on an adventure as unusual as it was ambitious, founding the nonprofit Aytimoun Yo association and moving to Haiti, a country with one of the lowest human development indices in the world, where already shocking socioeconomic conditions were further aggravated by the terrifying earthquake of January 2010.

Armed with courage and drive in abundance, Agostino and Lucia, their association members, and other supporters have achieved amazing results in a short space of time, opening a home on the border with the Dominican Republic for more than thirty orphaned or abandoned children (most of whom have been victims of all manner of violence) and ensuring them a decent life, safe from the dangers of life on the streets. Beside the home they have set up a school for the resident children and another forty from local families, who cannot afford the albeit minimal public school fees. Last but not least, the association has launched a farming project for the women of the village, who are granted plots of land of about 200 square meters to cultivate so they can earn enough income to maintain their children.

At the end of 2012, the Aytimoun Yo association experienced a difficult period in which, in a complicated and sometimes hostile political context, resources seemed to be running out. At that point it decided to up the ante, to "unpair the cards," with a project to expand the scheme to include a small business producing compost from organic and human waste, a cooking school, and a restaurant in Pedernales, just across the border in the Dominican Republic. After all, Lucia and Agostino are, first and foremost, gastronomes, as they themselves confess and as their degree certificates state, and it is gastronomy that drives them and their projects. Haiti is an extremely difficult country, arguably one of the most difficult in the world, so the fact that gastronomy can be a tool of emancipation in such a context is a signal of all the power it is capable of releasing—of liberating.

The stories of Lucia in Ventanilla and Aytimoun Yo in Haiti are completely different and refer to totally diverse historical, social, and cultural contexts. But they tell the same tale as the many other episodes I have related in this book. They are stories that valorize the meaning of work to defend small peasants and farmers and traditional produce, of education on quality, the demand for "good, clean, and fair," and the fight for social justice in the food system. They crown a reflection that began all those years ago with wine tastings in cellars in the Langa area of Piedmont and the reawakening of one's senses to appreciate goodness. Ultimately we have appreciated much more by "tasting reality," and we expect to appreciate much more still. I am sure that, through gastronomy, food will make us free, if it becomes *our* food once again, in every way extant and imaginable, according to culture and inclination. Because food is freedom.

# ACKNOWLEDGMENTS

First of all, I would like to thank my traveling companions: every single Slow Food collaborator with whom I have enjoyed infinite joys, hundreds of projects, many ideas, and lots of hard but enjoyable work (especially Chiara Cauda of Slow Food Editore for organizing work on this book, and Rinaldo Rava, a member of my office staff, for his precious help on the final sections on Peru, Colombia, and Mexico); all the members of the Slow Food association, past and present, who have helped us grow in local areas to be what we are and who represent us on a volunteer basis with undying passion; and most of all, the humanity of the Terra Madre communities who, besides welcoming and educating me, and making me happy, have performed a decisive role in building a network that has grown well beyond my wildest dreams.

A special thanks, finally, to Carlo Bogliotti, who has been by my side for more than ten years, elaborating and developing ideas, and putting them down on paper.